M000010006

"We live in extraordinary times that urgently call for a new paradigm of leadership. As Susan writes: 'Our internal conflicts carry over into all that we do.' It is self-evident that conflicted people produce conflicted results and a conflicted world. Leaders in every walk of life urgently need to get in touch with their own true self and bring that authenticity into all aspects of their lives. When they do, they and their organizations will thrive.

"Susan has spent decades learning and embodying yogic techniques and philosophy that enable us to connect with our unconflicted true self and bring it into the world in *all* of our actions. What she has uniquely done is to create a system that integrates this wisdom within the paradigm of leadership. Susan clearly lays out a novel approach applicable to leaders at every level of an organization, as well as across all sectors of society. This book is also for everyone who seeks to effectively be of genuine service to others, including business coaches, teachers, doctors, and lawyers, among others. We highly recommend this ground-breaking book to anyone looking to create extraordinary results with joy."

—Drs. Brian and Mary Nattrass, managing partners of Sustainability Partners, Batten Fellows of the Darden School of Business, and authors of *The Natural Step for Business* and *Dancing with the Tiger: Learning Sustainability Step by Natural Step*

"As a leadership speaker, business book author, and executive business coach who works with Fortune 100 companies and businesses around the world, I see *Inner Switch: 7 Timeless Principles to Transform Modern Leadership* as a novel contribution to the leadership field. Susan Freeman's methodology guides executives to navigate the complex landscape they work in. There will be receptivity for her methodology both in the United States and internationally, as leaders in many cultures will welcome advice on leveraging the wisdom of yoga to become more effective. Moreover, I am certain that executive coaches will want to include Susan's methodology in their toolkits as they work with their clients to help them be more open-minded, centered, and effective. Susan's book extends the way we lead from something we do to the way we show up."

—Rania H. Anderson, founder of The Way Women Work and author of *WE: Men, Women, and the Decisive Formula for Winning at Work* and *Undeterred: The Six Success Habits of Women in Emerging Economies*

"Reading *Inner Switch: 7 Timeless Principles to Transform Modern Leadership* is a life-changing experience. This book is such a gift and a breakthrough addition to the existing leadership literature.

"As founders and CEOs, my peers and I have been focused on traditional leadership teachings, such as how to create good metrics, brands, and cultures. We have avoided, to the great detriment of our organizations, teams, and our own growth, everything covered in *Inner Switch*. Instead of the traditional leadership books that focus on doing more, working harder, or changing other people, *Inner Switch* is like a wise spiritual teacher that helps you discover a new state of mind.

"If I'd read this book earlier in my career and understood how important it was for me to also address my spirit in order to improve my work, it would have made a dramatic improvement in my leadership. Although this book uses Western language so that it is universally accessible, it is at its essence a deeply spiritual approach to your personal growth, your level of consciousness, and developing your inner state as a leader. This book is for individuals who want to take their organizations to the next level and who are ready to elevate their consciousness, confront their limitations, and lead happier and more peaceful lives."

—**Elizabeth Dearborn Hughes,** cofounder and CEO, Davis College and Akilah College for Women, Rwanda

"In an ever-changing, complex global environment, leaders must be masters of transformation. This book explores the hidden truths behind what anyone who wishes to influence others with impact needs to know. As Susan Freeman wisely points out in *Inner Switch*, leaders are responsible for the quality of energy in an organization. Harmony, co-creation, and impact require leaders who are capable of self-modulation on a deep level. This book offers a blueprint for such development.

"I've known Susan since we attended Columbia Business School together. She, as a friend, has influenced my perspectives throughout my career. I am so proud she has written this book to bring her unique perspective and wisdom to a wide audience. When I read it, I recognized she is offering up a new way of doing business, one that is needed in these times. Every person who influences and leads others needs to read this book."

—**Masahiko Uotani**, president and group CEO, Shiseido Co. Ltd.

"I highly recommend Susan Freeman's spectacular book *Inner Switch: 7 Timeless Principles to Transform Modern Leadership*. I couldn't put it down. This extraordinary exploration of critical leadership competencies offers Eastern tools in Western language that every businessperson can relate to and easily apply. As a senior executive in a large and prominent value-based, member-centric organization, I find clearing my mind and actively managing my energy to be essential aspects of effectively leading teams and achieving success.

"In easy-to-digest and compelling language with useful case vignettes, this book explains both the scientific 'why' and the practical 'how' of incorporating these relaxation principles into your day and life. To bring out their best and guide them in fulfilling our mission of service to the public, I would love for all of our employees to read this work and practice these techniques. Undoubtedly, those who do will feel less stress, reduce friction in their working relationships, enhance their creativity, and generate best-in-class outcomes and results."

—**Marketa Wills**, Chief Medical Officer, Johns Hopkins HealthCare

"*Inner Switch: 7 Timeless Principles to Transform Modern Leadership* is a breakthrough milestone that literally changes the way we think about what leadership is. Susan Freeman's unique and cutting-edge approach goes beyond the Western viewpoint. It is grounded in practical Eastern techniques that help people learn about their inner energy and how to connect it to personal and professional effectiveness. The result is increased personal awareness along with the ability to integrate physical, psychological, and emotional contexts, which will have clear results on our judgment and ability to influence others. I have been open to learning much about mindfulness for over 20 years, and nowhere have I seen such related and complex concepts explained so beautifully.

"As an executive coach to senior organizational leaders in large corporations, I see this book as an invaluable resource for leaders who are committed to evolving their leadership capacities. It should be read and digested by leaders and coaches alike."

—**Maria Arnone**, executive coach

"A pleasure to read. By applying the art, science, and practice of yoga to everyday leadership situations, the author delivers on her claim to help with the inner switch of leadership. The book focuses on being open, learning by doing, and knowing how to let go of beliefs and habits that no longer serve you well. To do this, leaders must be present in the moment by actively leaning in to situations with body, mind, heart, and soul. Really being there. When leaders are so engaged, others seek connection with them and their energy. It is with this connection that the influence of their efforts is felt by others. Those who can embellish this connection to illuminate the talents of others ensure a shared experience for others to respond to with their talents and resources. The author's conversational style and exacting knowledge of the disciplines she uses to illustrate how contemporary ideas are part of yogic wisdom are coupled with poignant examples from her work and life experiences."

—**Stephen A. Stumpf**, professor of management, Franklin University Switzerland, and former Fred J. Springer Chair in Business Leadership, Villanova University (United States)

INNER
SWITCH

7 Timeless Principles to
TRANSFORM
MODERN LEADERSHIP

SUSAN S. FREEMAN

Entrepreneur Press®

The stories in this book are true. However, in the interest of protecting their privacy, some details about people and organizations have been altered to disguise their identities.

Entrepreneur Press, Publisher
Cover Design: Andrew Welyczko
Production and Composition: Eliot House Productions

This publication is designed to provide accurate and authoritative information in regard to the subject matter covered. It is sold with the understanding that the publisher is not engaged in rendering legal, accounting, or other professional services. If legal advice or other expert assistance is required, the services of a competent professional person should be sought.

Entrepreneur Press* is a registered trademark of Entrepreneur Media, Inc.

Library of Congress Cataloging-in-Publication Data
Names: Freeman, Susan S., author.
Title: Inner switch: 7 timeless principles to transform modern leadership / Susan S. Freeman.
Description: [Irvine]: [Entrepreneur Press], [2023] | Includes index. | Summary: "In a clear, linear, sequential system, highly regarded executive coach Susan S. Freeman lays out a transformational path for mainstream western business leaders through ancient yogic wisdom, and guides leaders to become better versions of themselves so that they can create positive change in their organizations" —Provided by publisher.
Identifiers: LCCN 2022049100 | ISBN 9781642011579 (trade paperback) | ISBN 9781613084670 (epub)
Subjects: LCSH: Leadership—Psychological aspects | Leadership—Religious aspects.
Classification: LCC HD57.7 .F743 2021 | DDC 658.4/092—dc23/eng/20221031
LC record available at https://lccn.loc.gov/2022049100

Printed in the United States of America

27 26 25 24   10 9 8 7 6 5 4 3 2 1

To all leaders who deserve this learning and the world that they will help co-create.

Contents

Foreword by Luis Coreano CEO, MAPP Technologies . . . .**xv**

Preface . . . .**xix**
    A Path of Self-Knowledge. xx
    A Path of Professional Discovery xxiv
    Building a New, Yoga-Inspired Approach
       to Leadership. xxv
    The Origins of Yoga xxvii

Introduction: Beyond Mindfulness . . . .**xxix**
    The Inner Switch™ Way. xxxi
    How to Use This Book xxxiii
    The Journey to Conscious, Embodied Leadership. . . xxxvi

CHAPTER 1

Open: Go Beyond Habit 1

What Does Work/Life Balance Truly Mean? 4

Living While Leading: Focusing on "How" Rather Than "What" 5

What If Leadership Isn't Just About What You're Doing? 7

The Root of What Disconnects Us Lies Within Us 10

Close-Mindedness Is Limiting and Stressful, Not Productive 12

That's Just How It Is—Or Is It? 14

When You Are Open, the Answers Reveal Themselves to You 15

Your Real Circle of Influence 15

Open to the One Who Is Observing 16

Cultivate Openheartedness 16

Have a Beginner's Mind 17

Opening Practices 19

CHAPTER 2

Learn: Reorient Your Focus **23**

Reorientation of Your Focus Is Necessary 24

Learning May Be More Than You Think It Is 27

Accountability Is Key to Successful Learning 29

The Five Hallmarks of Being-Based Leadership 30

Exercise to Experience Your Prana 34

The Effective Leader Works Within Their Circle of Influence 43

A Leader Must Take Radical Responsibility for
Their Emotions and Thought Patterns 45

CHAPTER 3

Let Go: Explore Your Edges **47**

The Body Is the Gateway to Transitioning from
Reactive to Responsive 51

What Is "Letting Go"? 54

Exploring Your Edge in Yoga as Training for Business and Life 55

Life Is Your Yoga Mat 58

The Letting Go Visualization Workout 64

The Seated Forward Bend: A Physical Practice of Letting Go 67

Rising Up by Letting Go 68

CHAPTER 4

Drop In: Shift from Doing to Nondoing **71**

How We Are Absent in the Present at Work 72

Break Out of Your Distortions to Drop into Your Presence. 75

Cultivate Your Body's Wisdom 76

How to Respond vs. React for Leadership Effectiveness 77

What a Piece of Work Are We! 79

The Anatomy of Our Energy System: The Five *Koshas*
or Dimensions of Awareness. 80

Connecting the *Koshas* to Leadership. 84

The Chakras: A Blueprint for Working with
Our Energy as Leaders 84

System Management: Your Breath Is the Key to Slowing
and Harnessing Your Mind. 88

Breathing Practices to Regulate Your State 90

The Practice of Dropping In 93

CHAPTER 5

Integrate: Live with Intention **101**

What Is Integration? 103

The Power of Embodied Knowledge. 105

Integration Occurs When We Move from Thinking and Doing
to Feeling and Being. 109

The Five Stages of Integration 110

Why Integration Is Central to Effective Leadership 112

Equanimity: An Additional, Significant Benefit of Integration 112

When Is It a Good Idea to Pause and Get Integrated?............ 113

Ayurvedic Wisdom: The Yogic Art of Living 115

20 Complementary Qualities of Experience to Balance........... 118

Taking Integration Forward 120

Yoga Nidra: The Sleep of the Yogis. 120

CHAPTER 6

Connect: Create Real Communication **125**

How to Create Real, Connected Communication. 129

Reactivity: The Number-One Impediment to Connection 130

Responses Are Truth, Reactions Are Lies. 130
Loving Leaders Create Connection 132
Creating Conscious, Compassionate Communication. 133
Establishing Resonance: Leading by
   Deliberately Amplifying Energy 137
Dissonance Must Be Addressed Early. 138
Elements of Team Building from a Vedic Perspective. 141
Connection Within a Team Enables Co-Creation 142
Ayurveda: A Leadership Hack for Meeting People
   "Where They Are". 144

CHAPTER 7

Illuminate: Become an Inner Switch Leader **147**
What Is a Remover of Darkness in a Leadership Context? 149
How Does Healthy Polarity Apply to Leaders? 151
An Inner Switch Leader Is Like a Self-Cleaning Oven. 154
Inner Switch Leaders Aim for Success Without Stress. 155
Inner Switch Leaders Step Back so Others Can Step Forward 157
How His Personal Transformation Enabled Kevin to
   Make a Companywide Impact 160
Key Principles for Becoming an Inner Switch Leader 165
Guidelines for Illuminating Conversations .167
Love May Be the Highest Aspiration of the Inner Switch Leader . . .167

Afterword **169**

APPENDIX

Designing a Regular Practice **173**

Resources **175**
Author's Website 175
Resources for *Yoga Nidra* 175
Resources for Ayurveda. 176
Resources for Clearing the Chakras 176

Endnotes. **177**

Acknowledgments..181

About the Author..185

Index 187

Foreword

I have been on a path to become a better human for some time. I see it as a never-ending journey that has great rewards for those who fully embrace it. Fortunately, I met Susan Freeman, who has been transformational to my evolution as a leader and as a person.

As we all know, leaders of organizations are always challenged with unknowns. Susan's approach was instrumental in helping me connect my body, mind, and all of my being. Our work together was aimed at me learning how to make an inner shift to gain mental agility. Through the framework she suggested, along with a variety of techniques that I practiced in between our sessions, I noticed things changing for me. As a technical leader, I became more connected to the interface of my mind-body and received a significant boost to my mental agility. The feeling of being connected inside oneself is very unique and powerful. I will say I feel complete in a way I previously had not.

I was tested as a CEO as never before in 2020 with the impact of COVID-19 on my team. It was the ultimate test of our resilience. Fortunately, my company did extremely well during the pandemic. We were able to win five significant programs and log record customer bookings. I believe that I had a true competitive advantage due to my clarity of mind and mental agility from our work together. During the pandemic, I was able to lean more into my inner game and that was the first time I truly noticed how much inner shift had occurred in me. While the world was under significant pressure caused by the pandemic and leaders everywhere were trying to cope, I had a different experience. I developed a significant amount of patience, became more conscious of my audience and my connection toward them, and showed the resilience as a leader that made my team be at ease. All of this was possible because of the work Susan and I had done together.

The beauty of this book is that it offers a clear roadmap for leaders of organizations who want to have a true competitive advantage within their industries. It provides leaders with the tools to develop mental agility at the deepest levels. When this takes place, they can connect at a deep level within themselves and radiate this energy to others in their world with a deeper sense of purpose. Susan has codified the secrets to what has been missing for me and I imagine for others as well. I hope that readers will enjoy the transformational process as much as I have.

—Luis Coreano CEO, MAPP Technologies

You are the sky.
Everything else—it's just the weather.[1]

—PEMA CHÖDRÖN

Preface

When the student is ready, the teacher will appear.

—ANCIENT PROVERB

As with so many things in our lives, we often can't see the threads of commonality weaving through diverse events except in retrospect. This was certainly the case with the events that led to the creation of this book, a project I've worked on for several years.

If you'd told me 25 years ago, when I first stepped onto a yoga mat, that one day I'd be writing a book on the intersection of leadership and yoga, I would have belly laughed. I was perfectly happy in my career as a vice president in a boutique executive search firm. The thought of writing on such a "soft" subject would have seemed misguided even as recently as a decade ago. Yoga was what I did outside the office.

For me, the practice of yoga started purely as an escape from the stresses of my daily life. I put it in the same category as going to the gym to stay fit and relieve tension, or reading a good book before bed to help me relax.

But what began as a means of distracting myself from my intense workday and physically unwinding after long hours spent grinding at my desk or taking meetings back-to-back gradually settled into a ritual of homecoming—a chance to return to myself.

Yoga subsequently transformed my personal life and my work, and I saw an opportunity to blend the seemingly disconnected worlds of yoga and leadership. This book is about the inner journey that can bring us better ways to lead and more joyful lives.

A Path of Self-Knowledge

I came to yoga seeking *something*. At the time, I didn't know what that was. When I was struggling to find my center in a hectic, complicated life, yoga was a refuge. My days were long, and I had a seemingly endless to-do list. I was transitioning between jobs, married to a man with a high-stress career of his own, and we were raising three young, energetic boys. Life in those days felt like a war zone, full of battles that needed to be fought. But later, I concluded that I had to stop "fighting" altogether. There was no enemy—just a life to be lived.

The seeds of this realization were planted on my yoga mat.

When my sons were young and giving them attention was an everyday necessity, I still committed to attending yoga classes several times a week that included stretching, breathing, and a few minutes of meditation. Of course, my coveted alone time was sometimes unattainable. However, my quality of life on days I was able to do yoga was noticeably better than on days when I didn't.

Yoga offered me a place to go when I wanted just to "be," not necessarily to "do" anything. It was the first place I felt real stillness—the sensation of the clock as having stopped. For a little more than an hour at a time, there was nowhere to go and nothing to do except be alive in my body. And for a woman with a life as complex as mine, stillness and timelessness felt like pure bliss.

There was nothing to think about except those few physical focal points related to arriving in each of the different poses. I would focus my attention entirely on my bodily sensations as my thoughts faded into the background. And in that not-thinking state, I became aware of a dimension that I had rarely inhabited previously and felt a connection to something I didn't feel anywhere else.

I felt at peace.

Soon yoga became a trusted and dependable retreat for me—a place where I could go and, for a period, be immersed in an entirely different world. I was able to depend on it. Yoga offered me a sense of serenity I couldn't experience anywhere else, nurtured me in ways I could not have predicted, and transformed the ground that had been a place for winning battles into a fertile soil for planting seeds of growth. What a discovery!

Just a few years after I started my regular yoga practice, a great teacher appeared to me following an accident: my own body. A scale fell on my foot in a store while I was grocery shopping, giving me a contusion and fracture. I took care of the fracture and swollen, black-and-blue foot with a boot and the routine rest, ice, and elevation, and thought nothing more of it. But when I continued to experience burning pain at the site of the injury long after the expected six-week recovery period, I had to seek additional medical attention.

My teacher had arrived.

After a number of tests, I was diagnosed with reflex sympathetic dystrophy (RSD), or causalgia. RSD, now more commonly called complex regional pain syndrome (CRPS), is a disease of the autonomic nervous system (ANS), which is responsible for the involuntary regulation of our bodily functions, such as our heartbeat and respiration. The ANS includes both the sympathetic nervous system (SNS), where the physiological "fight-or-flight" stress response is activated and maintained, and the parasympathetic nervous system (PSNS), through which the opposite "relaxation" response occurs.

CRPS alters the sympathetic response in a painful limb in such a way that pain signals are continuously being produced at the site of a trauma long after an injury has healed. The body is essentially hijacked into producing a pain response that feels far worse than the initial trauma and must be endured long after the injury has technically healed.

When my foot was damaged, my ANS, normally running in the background of my consciousness, suddenly pushed its way to the forefront and made itself the center of my world. Almost all I thought of was pain and my hope of relief from pain. But there was no relief, and I could see no way out.

After multiple medical consults; taking a series of medications that made me feel loopy, forgetful, and fatigued; and receiving 16 injections of a nerve-blocking anesthetic, I was still experiencing horrific pain—it was as if my foot was literally on fire. I would sit for hours and often tried to sleep with my foot wrapped in ice packs.

I felt devastated when my doctors told me they had done everything they could and racked my brain for solutions. If I couldn't cure this condition, my life would be unlivable. I seemed destined to suffer serious depression—or worse. The path ahead looked bleak.

How can someone begin to heal herself when the professional healers are unable to help? That was the question before me. I hoped that yoga might help me to answer it.

Fortunately, I already had a cursory knowledge of yoga's benefits. Through yoga, I had learned to become a witness to my discomfort in a pose. When we are able to step back mentally and witness our sensations, including those that feel uncomfortable during either movement or the holding of a pose, we realize that *we* are not the discomfort. We are separate from it. I speculated that improving my ability to do this might somehow enable me to better tolerate my pain.

Developing this capacity of neutral observation was my initial intention, but I discovered that yoga provided me with so much more than a way to separate from my pain.

After five years of suffering, I leaned further into my yoga practice, trusting that the yoga mat would offer me a space for solace and healing that is absent in Western treatment. Because CRPS is maintained by the SNS and aggravated by fight-or-flight triggers, I figured, *why not try to activate my PSNS instead?*

I decided I would learn how to *consciously* use my yogic practice to activate the relaxation response. Overjoyed when the pain slowly began to resolve, I was convinced I should keep going. My pain flare-ups became the barometer of my practice and made me want to continue to strengthen my relationship with yoga.

As I developed a more in-depth knowledge of yoga, I learned just how much had been codified by teachers. I came to learn about *yoga nidra*, commonly known as yogic sleep, a technique wherein the PSNS is activated while the practitioner is conscious and awake. Finally, I came to appreciate the importance of good knowledge to accompany my practice. Then something else that felt magical happened.

Gradually, my practice revealed to me a deeper level of self-knowledge. I came to realize that the lessons I was learning on the mat while healing my body—especially finding stillness in movement and ease in discomfort—were translatable to my everyday experiences. Standing in lines, dealing with my kids when they acted up, multitasking at the office, driving in traffic—each of these experiences became a new "yoga mat" for me, another place where I could practice my yogic skills and perceptions.

As I drew my attention inward, I discovered an awareness that had previously eluded me. I grew more attuned to myself and those around me and grew increasingly conscious of how my thoughts and energy influenced my interactions with others. When I began to understand and experience my true self, I began to understand my relationships with other people at a much different level and came to appreciate how my energetic presence affected them.

As I learned to quiet my cognitive mind, my pain gradually dissipated and eventually disappeared altogether. I was able to stop taking medication to mask the symptoms of CRPS. In addition, I found myself becoming a more authentic and skillful leader. Serendipitously, I found connections between elements from my healing path and what my business coaching clients needed to be their best in their personal and professional lives.

A Path of Professional Discovery

The two parallel paths of my life began to merge. I had trained as an ontological coach, rooting myself in the theory of "being." In this approach, the coach looks for coherence between an individual's body, emotions, and language—their way of being—as a means of helping a client shift behavior. I now saw novel possibilities for how yogic principles shifted my own perceptions and therefore might translate into the realm of helping clients through my leadership coaching.

My clients exhibited many of the same stressors and embodied much of the same suffering as I had due to my painful foot, although bringing different problems to me for discussion. When it came to assisting these business executives in improving their decision making and overcoming blockages or extreme reactivity, there appeared to be a clear path forward—and it was not one either they or I had been taught in graduate school or another professional training program. Many of them were as disconnected from themselves as I had been from myself before my CRPS, and I was intrigued by using the principles of yoga to teach them to form deep self-connections, even if they had never been on a yoga mat.

The two main questions I needed to answer at that juncture were "Can you build the bridge between yoga and leadership effectively?" and "Are you courageous enough to take your Western-educated clients into this realm of experience?" I say *courageous* because I worried that I would face skepticism or even ridicule. Yoga's benefits are real but not as easy to calculate on a spreadsheet as income and expenses.

Yoga places significant emphasis on accessing sensations in the body, and sensations are just information and energy. A new way of thinking about leadership is as an embodied experience. Yoga has implications for our physical and emotional well-being and therefore for our leadership. This became evident to me when yoga began to positively impact my performance in business. By then, I had developed both a nuanced understanding of yoga and a good manner of practice.

Yoga taught me how to consciously engage the PSNS when I felt pressured. Similarly, effective leaders must have the capacity to be present and relaxed in their bodies while they are working toward their goals. This too requires deliberate, conscious activation of the PSNS.

An inability to access the body—to have a physical and emotional experience of our own energy—doesn't just prevent us from being effective; it also stops us from connecting to others in our workplaces and homes and deriving joy from it. Self-connection is an important missing capacity for many leaders. Fortunately, the practice of yoga postures and breath work can help us free our energy and minds so that we may form this sort of connection and develop presence.

While most leaders mercifully do not need to have scales dropped on their feet as I did, they do have to face challenges that are similarly stressful. Take the COVID–19 pandemic: All the adjustments that had to be made to keep employees and customers safe for the duration of the pandemic are an example of a scenario that demands a lot from leaders. But there was only one choice: adapt or quit.

The word *business* pretty much says it all—there is a lot of *busy*-ness in doing business. Lots of meetings. Lots of phone calls and Zoom chats. Lots of reading, travel, and decisions to be made. Lots of responsibility to customers, employees, and investors. Lots of "time sucks" and personal sacrifice. And too few hours to manage everything without adequate support and structure. Leaders can treat their employees terribly and treat themselves worse in trying to get everything done. They may try to override their body's need for stillness to counterbalance their push, push, pushing, but this approach is not ideal. The better solution is to practice the one thing we can control: self-regulation.

That's what this book is about: the inward journey that makes us better leaders.

Building a New, Yoga-Inspired Approach to Leadership

Although yoga was transforming my life, I didn't choose to directly incorporate its benefits into my coaching right away. At first, I was concerned that the leaders who were my clients—distinctly Western heads of corporations and team leaders—would recoil at the thought of incorporating ancient Eastern philosophy and practices into their daily regimens. At the time, mindfulness techniques were not on the radar in corporate training programs. I only stealthily started introducing my clients to a yogic approach to leadership when I saw they were open to transforming their leadership capabilities in novel ways.

Over the past decade, I have directly taught ancient yogic principles to the clients I serve through my executive coaching company. I often work with founders, C-level executives, and teams in high-growth, entrepreneurial organizations. Once we have built trust in our relationship, I find they are primed for such an innovative approach and receptive to new concepts.

When I began incorporating Eastern teachings into my coaching, I emphasized the yogic approach of *inward focus* first, without naming it as such. To my surprise and delight, the more I included this practice in the training I offered, the more positively my clients responded. In fact, many of them specifically began to ask for it in our sessions! As I slowly and gently guided them through yoga-like experiences "off the mat," they described experiencing a sense of deep calm and stillness. They were sensing a subtle, yet profound, new energy. Their vocal tone and pace of speech relaxed; their mental, emotional, and physical clarity increased; and they became more aware of their bodies. They were able to focus on essential questions with more ease. They were also able to resolve troubled relationship conflicts, not only at work, but also at home. What quickly unfolded surprised me: My clients reported both increased effectiveness *and* joy. Apparently, I had tapped into something that people were yearning for and they did not previously know what that was.

As my clients increasingly sought out this aspect of our work together, my instincts about the application of yoga to business activities were validated. One leader called me from across the country and asked me to help her implement a yogic centering technique as she was about to enter into contract negotiations for a $40 million project. (Her negotiations were successful.) Another asked me to help him do the same prior to a pitch to raise capital—a task he prevailed at on this occasion, although he previously had been unsuccessful.

Since then, I've tested and refined my understanding of how to incorporate the timeless wisdom of yoga to business. From experimenting with individuals, I moved to engaging with teams. In both contexts and multiple scenarios, the results were reliable and inspiring.

The Origins of Yoga

Much of the ancient wisdom that underlies the practices yoga practitioners embrace to this day was codified in India by a sage named Patanjali, who lived at some point between the second century BCE and the fifth century CE. Not much is known about him—not even if he was one man or several whose instructions got conflated over the centuries. The ancient teachings of Patanjali's tradition, known as the Vedas, go back even further than he—more than 5,000 years. They were orally transmitted until he set them down on parchment.

In the East, Patanjali is honored for creating the *Yoga Sutras,* a collection of 185 texts written in Sanskrit on the theory and practice of yoga. This was handed down through various lineages of teachers for thousands of years. However, as yoga migrated to those of us residing here in the West in recent decades, much of the deeper meaning of his words has been lost in translation. Many of those who are practicing yoga in North America and Europe today learn only "snippets" of the true teaching from their instructors at the local gym or yoga studio. And most who partake will not go on to explore what they are missing. The growth of their practices is stunted.

Some Westerners are put off by their perception that yogic principles are religious teachings. Although yoga does share many philosophical undertones with some Eastern religions, I have come to learn that this body of work transcends any and all specific religious traditions. The teachings of this approach to living belong to the world at large.

Although most of my clients enjoy learning information derived from the yogic tradition I have studied, this book is the first place where I have revealed in written form the deep structure that informs my work. I have done this so that others who may not be able to receive coaching from me can benefit from this universal wisdom. I have also attempted to codify my understanding of these teachings in a manner that is relevant to a modern business audience.

For clarity's sake, let us distinguish here between ancient Eastern wisdom and what is experienced now in many current cultures. Even in the East today, as emerging economies rush to compete and pursue a path of rapid industrialization, many people are distanced from the jewels of ancient wisdom handed down by their forebears. But in its purest form, yoga is being kept alive in ashrams and in institutes of yoga, both in India and in other countries. We will draw from these traditional teachings in our discussions. I am offering you an opportunity to bridge the ancient wisdom of the East with the kind of practical strategic blueprint demanded by the West.

This book represents my personal integration of knowledge inherent to a vast number of fields. Its overall guiding structure comes from yoga. I have drawn from numerous teachers of yoga, who are experts in many specialties. Yoga includes technical, philosophical, dietary, and lifestyle approaches. Additionally, I have integrated material drawn from the fields of psychology, coaching, and leadership, to name just a few. It is a privilege to present a distillation of ideas and experiences that offer leaders a fresh opportunity to blend multiple modalities in a modern way. This book has been constructed to appeal to Western leaders through a linear sequential structure, which is atypical of the way yogic wisdom is usually taught.

You might be like my clients: curious about yoga yet put off by what you see as the "pretzel poses" that often pass for it. Or you may not see yourself as someone who would go to a yoga seminar or intensive, much less visit an ashram.

Yes, yoga *can* involve poses. Yet it is so much more than that! As a teacher of mine once said: "You can't stretch your way into enlightenment."

The years during which this book was gestating taught me many things. With respect to leadership, I know that leaders can and must first learn to be human presences. *Then* they become remarkable leaders. It doesn't work the other way around. A leadership presence that begins inside us can be extended to all whom we influence and inspire to do excellent and meaningful work. But embodying such a presence is a process, not an event. We need to develop, stretch, and evolve ourselves as leaders every single day so we can rise to meet the moment.

Take heart. This book isn't aimed at getting you on a yoga mat (although that may occur). My goal is that your response to yoga will go, as mine did, from *that's woo-woo!* to *wahoo!*

Let the journey begin.

Introduction
Beyond Mindfulness

Where wisdom reigns there is no conflict
between thinking and feeling.[1]

—CARL JUNG

Leaders have an opportunity and, dare I say, a responsibility to influence and change the world. Those who lead in organizations naturally impact employees and teams, clients and customers, vendors, stockholders, and other stakeholders, so being leaders offers them a robust opportunity for creating potentially far-reaching societal transformation. Effective leadership is important.

The competencies associated with effective leadership are well recognized. These include, yet are not limited to, being visionary, strategic, decisive, intelligent, loyal, disciplined, determined, persistent, and good at communication. Also desired and admired are qualities like insight, resilience, integrity, good judgment, and wisdom. But although these are essential components of leadership, they aren't enough on their own to draw people close to us or inspire them to work passionately to fulfill a vision and strategy. Nor do they promote joyful collaboration and personal well-being. These added distinctions are what fascinates me.

Our happiness and health suffer when we place the honoring of achievements above our own humanity and ignore the omnipresent energy that animates and sustains us. With this approach, we are likely to damage ourselves and others and destroy some relationships along the way to success. Our internal conflicts carry over into all that we do.

As an executive business coach, I have observed the cracks that appear when the demands on leaders outpace their personal and leadership competencies. People are often promoted based on the technical and functional skills and experience they have gained from being in a particular role or industry. The better they perform, the more they are rewarded with promotions, with little or no emphasis on having the requisite leadership competencies for the next level. But early career successes built on operational know-how are no longer adequate when the leader's role increasingly demands self-awareness and blending with those whom the leader relies on to realize their organizational vision and set goals. Leaders who lack these skills often get stuck, creating heartache for individuals and organizations alike.

A leader with an outdated internal operating system is soon at a disadvantage. Because of the rapid pace of the contemporary world, stagnation in leadership development is synonymous with falling behind. It is often at this junction where leaders seek out leadership development and coaching, not knowing that what they *really* are seeking is to develop their capacity for self-regulation—the so-called inner game.

What many traditional leadership-training programs fail to emphasize is that *all* leaders need to continuously develop themselves as human beings. In fact, as leaders we need to understand that our teams, divisions, and organizations—and families—can only grow to the degree that we improve our own self-awareness. The further we rise in the ranks and the more responsibility we have for others, the more of an imperative there is for us to grow as people.

That's where making the *inner switch* comes in. Yogic centering and presencing practices based on ancient Vedic wisdom are a reliable, time-tested means of personal development.

I would argue that in the West it is only in the past decade or so that there has been widespread interest in increasing the connection to our own fully embodied presence. During this time, however, this has been counterbalanced by increasing technological forces that draw us away from being present. The world we live in is increasingly disruptive and destabilizing, both mentally and emotionally. We are paying a high price for our use of technology. Despite being more electronically connected than ever, with a smartphone in nearly every pocket, most of us have never felt less "in the moment," and our technological disconnection from our true selves increases our disconnection from others.

If we are not present within our own being, how can we be present for others or engage in co-creative conversations and activities with them? Although the internet and social media have the potential to be a force for greater global connection, our relationships today are too often filtered through computer screens and character counts, devoid of authentic human contact.

Something needs to shift so that we can feel energetically alive and be available when we are leading a team or an organization. An evolution of our consciousness is required if our leadership is to be meaningful to those we have the privilege of leading and for our presence to be relevant to their daily endeavors. Should we consider counting ourselves among the people we lead?

The Inner Switch™ Way

Masterful leaders are teachers, but they are more than that. Teachers often work to change others but not necessarily to change themselves. Leaders who have made the inner switch change themselves *so* that they can influence others. They can then transmit teachings in a way that resonates. They can transcend the words they speak by managing their interior landscape: their mindset, emotions, and energy. They connect to their own nonreactive inner energy first, so they can connect, influence, and ultimately co-create with others. Such a leader can incorporate internal harmony into virtually any activity, from doing business to being the head of a family. Such a person presents a truly distinctive approach when they become an Inner Switch Leader.

This kind of leadership inspires and improves the quality of life for those who are working with us. When this happens, the activity in a workplace isn't just about getting the work done. Instead, our places of work become a laboratory of living, sensing, and connected beings. Although invisible to the eye, we know when this energy is absent. Without this type of embodied style, leaders may attempt to get efficient results through demanding, dominating, or authoritative behavior. But this doesn't inspire others or increase their creativity—in fact, it does just the opposite—so any improvements are usually ineffective or short-lived.

The new style of leadership you will read about in this book occurs when leaders are relaxed, open-minded, and intentional—when they welcome new ideas and are ready to co-create with others. When leaders integrate intellect and feeling, they experience a whole new level of engagement and productivity and can help others get there, too. Everyone involved feels accepted, trusted, and recognized for being genuinely who they are when these leaders are around. Although the power of human presence has always existed, it has not usually been a focus of leadership, with rare exceptions.

The kind of leadership transformation I am envisioning for you is perhaps best illustrated by Salvador Dalí's classic paintings *The Persistence of Memory* and *Melting Watch*, in which the artist portrayed limp, dissolving clocks. The powerful visual is a metaphor signifying the fleeting nature of time. Dalí's works challenge viewers to shift their attention from the past and future to the here and now.

Feeling ourselves melting into the moment like one of Dalí's clocks is an experience that yoga is perhaps uniquely qualified to promote. The term *yoga* may be translated as "yoke" or "unite." Through a variety of modalities, including movement and meditation, yoga offers us a means of yoking our individual consciousness to a universal consciousness, transcending its simple physical poses.

When practiced in a business context, yoga allows us to detach from the reactive, programmed conditioning of the mind. Fearful memories from the past and anxieties about the future are unconscious distortions that distract us from an experience of things as they are in *this* moment. Your recognition that leadership occurs *here* and *now* could permanently and positively disrupt everything you do moving forward if you allow it to guide your thoughts and actions.

This book is *not* about how to improve leadership as it has been traditionally defined. That has been done repeatedly. It *is* about extending the notion of leadership from simply a way of acting in the world to a way of *being* within us that we share with the world. Our actions are always initiated from a particular way of being, but we usually are not aware of how the quality of our being precedes our doing. We need to grasp this, as favoring being over doing is essential for our health, well-being, and happiness as humans. And it's good for productivity and results as well!

How to Use This Book

In *Inner Switch: 7 Timeless Principles to Transform Modern Leadership* I aim to present a distinctive approach to leadership in a manner you can learn, practice, and readily embody. As you read successive chapters, you will begin to intentionally use your personal state more and more to influence your leadership interactions. This method will give you the ability to clarify your vision for your organization and transmit it to others, inspiring and influencing them with your presence. This is not a spiritual path; it is a practical one—and it's never been more important for leaders than it is today.

When leaders make a habit of focusing inward on themselves and their internal state before making a decision, holding a meeting, making a phone call, walking down a hallway, or interacting with staff, they become more open and receptive. They leave the defended structure of their reactive ego mind, having developed a capacity to disengage from fearful narratives derived from past experiences, as well as from their anxieties about the future. They are able to reduce conflict in the workplace because they have done so first within themselves.

Those who have adopted this method report feeling unburdened and being able to choose just the right action at the right time. They have become co-creative partners with others.

Equally important, their stress is reduced. Over the years, I have repeatedly heard not only that their companies have benefited from this approach, but also that the leaders I coached enjoyed improved physical well-being—some lost weight, some eliminated long-standing insomnia. Others stopped needing medication for high blood pressure.

In every case, the bodies of these high-performance leaders reflected the mental and emotional transformation they experienced inside themselves. As this happened, the manner in which they engaged with others in the world changed in unexpected and welcome ways. Their inner growth was reflected in the outer growth of their organizations. Things improved in a similar manner at home with their families.

How then do you make the inner switch? Mindfulness is a necessary component, yet alone it is not enough. A deeper style of leadership is required. You must develop skills and take radical personal responsibility for how you manage your internal energetic state. This is essential to increase your capacity to show up in the moment, bring your best self to the matter at hand, and connect with other people at a mental, emotional, and energetic level.

Yoga is not a state of being. It is a practice that can transform the practitioner when it is done regularly. Similarly, leadership, when practiced with an intentional structure, offers the practitioner an abundance of significant positive changes. This is a skill sorely needed in our world today, where in every single moment we are deluged with stimulation that draws our attention and disrupts our focus.

In this book, I outline seven principles drawn from ancient yogic wisdom that can help you shift from unconscious reactor to conscious responder and lead others to do the same. Each chapter teaches one principle, explaining why and how to practice it on your own:

- *Open.* Embrace the beginner's mind, which is open to the new and unknown.
- *Learn.* Understand the limitations of your mind and its reliance on conditioning.
- *Let go.* Move from stressful reactivity to stimuli toward conscious responding.
- *Drop in.* Experience the way of being that arises from neutral observation.
- *Integrate.* Bring body, mind, heart, and being together to act spontaneously in balance in the present, as we become the observer.
- *Connect.* Tune into your internal state of harmony before communicating with others.
- *Illuminate.* Cultivate a space where others may release their unconscious reactivity so everyone can respond powerfully in the present.

I use modern vocabulary and voice to share concepts that have been time-tested over several millennia and are now specifically reframed in the domain of leadership. My promise to you is that these secrets will teach you how to transform your working relationships from conflict-creating, stress-inducing, goal-oriented, reactive struggles into harmonious, joyous, effective, and responsive partnerships. You will learn how to stay calm, be resourceful, and confidently respond with compassion and equanimity, even when you're under pressure from external forces. You will experience a deeper sense of fulfillment and joy from your work and see opportunities that were previously hidden from you.

You will feel more confident that you have the right motivations and therefore can trust that you are doing the right thing for the right reason. In time, if you practice your yogic techniques while doing business, the presence you experience while doing the practices will transfer to more and more moments, and you'll come to experience more of the now throughout your everyday life. In so doing, a new, healthy mind-body relationship will be created within you. You, in turn, can share your authentic presence with others.

For me, this presence is where true leadership lives.

There is an order to the presentation of these principles, which, as a unit, become steps in a sequence, and your progress in performing them requires you to develop the skills in this order. However, it is important to note that we all go in and out of states that each of them is designed to address throughout the day. The key question becomes, can you sense your energy, assess your state, and adjust it as necessary in the moment? This becomes the ongoing practice that will sustain, nourish, and challenge you. When you are aware of your inner state and become adept at this, you'll be able to do these steps in the matter of a breath or two.

Certain leadership moments may be best viewed from the vantage point of different chapters. For example, if you are having difficulty seeing the perspective of someone on your team, read Chapter 1, "Open."

If you find it difficult to embrace different perspectives, read Chapter 2, "Learn."

If you feel as if you are running in circles, unable to do anything to alleviate the burnout, read Chapter 3, "Let Go."

When you need to have a high-stakes, challenging conversation with a colleague, read Chapter 4, "Drop In."

When you have a complex set of tasks requiring multiple initiatives and conversations, or are in a new role, read Chapter 5, "Integrate."

When you want to be truly heard and the relationship depends on it, read Chapter 6, "Connect."

Lastly, when you are ready to take your life and leadership practice to the level of full embodiment, harmony, co-creativity, and joy, read Chapter 7, "Illuminate."

The Journey to Conscious, Embodied Leadership

A leadership presence that begins inside us can be extended to all whom we influence. This is always a process, not an event. We need to develop, stretch, and evolve ourselves as leaders every single day. Transformation from unconscious leadership to aware and awakened leadership can be accomplished through a sequential, linear process. The catalyst we need to begin is already inside us with this energy that we can rediscover and then share. This form of leadership doesn't rely on power. It doesn't diminish anyone so that someone else can be elevated. Instead, it creates space for everyone to self-express and co-create most effectively.

Importantly, this approach kindles self-motivation in any group guided by an awakened and personally transforming leader. The leader uses their presence to create confidence in the group's ability to envision and achieve a shared goal. In the process, all the team members learn to access their dormant powers. A leader who can integrate intellect with intuition and compassion sets a standard that others will aspire to follow and develop for themselves.

We are discussing the journey to conscious, embodied leadership. In this way of leading, leaders certainly focus on external goals and their efforts to accomplish them, but *only* after they are connected to the omnipresent source of harmony within. This increases the likelihood of achieving their goals *and* improves the happiness and satisfaction of the leader and the team because it fosters creativity and co-creation.

The customary analytics we track when we do business, such as revenue, income, expenses, growth rate, employee retention, employee engagement, and so forth, continue to be tracked. However, as we move from the coarse level of business leadership to a more subtle level, other metrics need also be considered. Human beings are complicated: Our thoughts, feelings, and bodies alternate between rational and irrational impulses. Therefore, any interchange between humans has the potential to go in an infinite number of directions. The trajectory depends on our leadership presence.

What we can rely on is our energy. We are always emitting energy, but are we aware of the quality of the energy we are transmitting to others? For leaders, this requires communication that is not only verbal, but also connected to and integrated with the heart. Such leadership creates an energetic communion, which is the essence of yoga. Taking responsibility for the energy we bring to every situation increases the probability of a desirable outcome. Subtle leadership requires that we master this by example and then invite others to do the same. This is the vital difference associated with this approach.

By working *within yourself first* to remedy the imbalances that arise in your body and mind, you can be more mindful and ultimately develop the inner presence that results in true influence—power that flows but is not forced. As this new kind of leader, you can use your professional life as the motivation to achieve success *and* cultivate consciousness. When you do, you will bring this harmony into your life—no matter who you are with, where you are, or what you are doing. It will affect not only you, but also everyone you influence. The impact can be nothing short of transformational.

You may be wondering how long it will take. Development of mastery goes on throughout our lives, yet some benefits will accrue immediately upon the conscious practice of each principle. This requires an openness to learning something new and a willingness to leave behind things that once served us but no longer produce results or create joy.

The invitation is to appreciate that we are not separate from nature or from those around us. We aim to leave our organizations, communities, and families better than we found them. We have always wanted to do better *and* be better leaders; we simply haven't understood the mechanism for transforming our behavior until now. Developing the capacity for conscious, perhaps even enlightened leadership offers us a refreshing opportunity to do so.

I believe that every person who desires this capacity can develop it. *In fact, it is already within you just waiting to be activated.* You can't get it from outside yourself; it originates and must be cultivated within. When you do, you will have access to an internal landscape that offers clarity, confidence, insight, and presence. Imagine how good you will feel when this is what you readily share with others!

CHAPTER 1

Open
Go Beyond Habit

Everybody thinks of changing humanity, and nobody
thinks of changing himself.

—LEO TOLSTOY

The dream of the average leader in the Western world is to be influential, someone who can inspire and guide people to achieve their desired outcomes. We've been taught to believe that an emotional payoff comes from accomplishment, so if we aren't getting satisfaction, most of us will either change our actions or redouble our efforts and urge others to do the same. The trouble is that this outward-oriented approach can be very draining for us and for those we are leading. Our attention can easily become fully consumed by our attempts to manage the people, places, and things around us.

To achieve our objectives, each of us has a menu of actions we turn to from habit: our favorite tactics and hacks. And given the common preoccupation with appearing to have all the answers and be invulnerable, we may expend precious time and energy on defending the rightness of our point of view, beliefs, and desires. This serves to entrench us in our habits.

Really, it's no wonder that organizational life is full of failed experiments and unhappy people working themselves to the bone.

Dug-in leaders may be surprised to find that everyone around them isn't onboard with their plans, which can reinforce their sense of needing to work harder and longer themselves. Those who feel like they're missing out on things that matter feel this way because they're trying to keep pace on a veritable hamster wheel of activity.

Does any of this sound familiar to you?

Working hard in an effort to control outcomes so that you can feel good about yourself and impress people is a trap. Our world is volatile, uncertain, complex, and ambiguous.[1] Your ability to grow your business through teamwork and delegation may fail in ways you won't see coming. The recent global pandemic; ongoing technological revolutions; job losses due to globalization, automation, and artificial intelligence; and climate change and the political, economic, and human disruptions associated with it are rapidly altering how everyone does business. You will be highly stressed if you feel that achievement under these (or any other) conditions all comes down to you and your individual contribution!

There are drawbacks to leading by exertion and control. Under this type of leadership, employees often become discouraged and will leave an organization. When asked the reasons for their departure, they will complain about a lack of direction, micromanagement, or a "sweatshop culture." But they may not admit to being discouraged until after they hand in their resignation.

Among the biggest problems I see among the leaders I coach are their use of reactivity and force. Do you often, or ever, feel like you are putting out fires that are cropping up around you instead of making progress toward a positive vision? That's *reactivity*. Do you sometimes feel like you must push people to make things happen? That's *force*. If you are a habitually reactive or forceful leader, it is highly likely that you encounter stress and conflict as you conduct business every day. And your habitually stressful and conflicted style is probably spilling over into your personal life and affecting your health and relationships. Leaders whose styles are reactive and forceful often suffer from insomnia, hypertension, weight gain, and other physical symptoms.

Eventually, something gives.

In this book, we're going to look at leadership and how we can get things done from a new angle, the perspective of true self-connection. My contention is that before any of us can genuinely influence the behavior of others, we must learn to influence ourselves and shift our inner state. I invite you to consider that your ability to lead does not derive from what you do or say to persuade or motivate anyone. Rather, it comes from how you modulate and experience your own energy. It is a matter of *feeling and being* as opposed to *thinking and doing*.

The first step is to cultivate openness. Open your mind to possibility. Open to your inner experience of yourself. Open to connection with others. Open to the newness of every moment.

No matter how difficult or easy it seems, every moment holds an opportunity.

LEADERSHIP IN ACTION
How Alan Turned a Terrible Sales Meeting into a Five-Figure Deal

Alan, a sales executive in the high-end B2B arena, had been my client for less than a month when I got a happy call from him. "You'll never believe what just happened," he said. "I was in a sales meeting with the chief procurement officer at a medical center. This guy was in a fury as the meeting began. He was gruff, outspoken, and even bullying in the way he spoke to me, saying, 'We aren't going to spend the kind of money you're looking for, if that's what you're thinking.' But a few minutes later, there was an incredible turnaround."

Alan thought fast. He realized he'd have to leave the meeting right then if no sale was possible. Or he had another option, one he'd been working on lately: He could try to use his own energy to shift the energy of his prospective customer.

And that is what he did. He took some slow, deep breaths, centered himself, looked the man in the eyes, and then calmly yet firmly took charge of the conversation. He didn't try to change the customer. Instead, he focused on centering himself as we had been practicing in our first few sessions. In less than a minute, the procurement officer softened his stance. As a result, Alan went on to have an impactful conversation with the man, who purchased equipment worth $50,000 before the appointment ended.

What Does Work/Life Balance Truly Mean?

I often hear leaders yearning for the proverbial work/life balance. They believe there ought to be a way to create more time—all while choosing to work 18 hours a day. They are torn between honoring their commitments to their work, their families, and themselves. Are they seeking balance so they can give more at work or at home? Or are they seeking to replenish their bodies and minds so they can feel satisfied instead of drained? Are they hoping to find more meaning in their lives, both at work and outside it?

Implicit in this approach is the belief that how we live and how we work are at opposite ends of a spectrum and are equally important. *The radical proposition of this book is that our way of being while living and working are one and the same. Who we truly are does not change regardless of where we are or what we are doing.*

The work/life balance we seek is to be in harmony with ourselves in every moment, so we can experience innate joy in the journey of living as well as leading. Reactive leaders often get so caught up in defending the status quo that they cause themselves distress. For example, a leader who doesn't delegate will quickly become imbalanced through overwork. In the meantime, their colleagues won't learn to take on new responsibilities and grow their capacities. The result is that the growth of others becomes suppressed while the leader becomes depressed!

Successful leaders need to learn to feel whole and balanced within themselves. *Less striving and driving permits more thriving.* Successful leadership is not about doing more—it's about doing less forcing and reacting. If you stop forcing results and reacting with fear and negativity to your circumstances, you will be able to direct your energy toward replenishment and it will feel good.

Living While Leading: Focusing on "How" Rather Than "What"

The real solution to your desires lies dormant within you, not outside you. When you open yourself, you can then inspire openness in others. Being open is an opportunity to discover ways to promote your own inner harmony. *It is only when you experience inner harmony that you will be able to communicate, co-create with, and lead others.*

Seeking a quick fix or spending most of your time trying to figure out "how" to get what you want from others may perhaps get results, but the whole process will be so distasteful and alienating that you will create stress and disharmony within yourself and possibly for others. *How you are being, communicating, and showing your presence as you get where you need to go is as important as the goal itself.*

LEADERSHIP IN ACTION

How Theresa Navigated from Doubt to Decisiveness and Won a Seven-Figure Client

Theresa is the founder and CEO of a financial organization. She is a brilliant and successful leader, but, like many others with whom I have worked, she often struggles with self-doubt. When we met, it was clear to me that one of her great strengths was her creative and innovative thinking—she saw possibilities that others usually did not. The problem was that she felt awkward about this, often finding it difficult to connect and engage with others effectively.

Once we identified that what was getting in the way was Theresa's belief that there was a certain way successful leaders did things, and she opened her mind to doing things her own way, she saw new possibilities for herself. Until then, believing that she "ought" to be different or better at doing one thing than another often got in the way of her expressing and attempting what she was capable of doing well to her colleagues and clients.

She was still nervous, so we practiced her becoming present to herself and noticing what she was experiencing inside—what moods, emotions, and sensations happened as she imagined herself in a meeting with a prospective client. When she had a direct experience of this later in an actual sales meeting, she felt comfortable with her own approach and spoke to the client from her current moment—not from her fears or worries about what had happened in the past.

The result was that she opened up a co-creative possibility during the conversation, and her prospective client immediately noted how this discussion was different from those with other executives with whom she had met. Theresa's newfound openness resulted in her winning a seven-figure piece of business.

The most effective way to awaken as a leader is through cultivating the quality of openness. Openness is the gateway to creating receptivity in yourself to others and in them to you. Leaders who lack an internal practice to open themselves energetically create conflict with others. Their behaviors originate from habits, fears, anxiety, or ego-based desires for control. Others can sense that these leaders do not truly care for them as people. They do not feel valued or appreciated by them and will not use their creative potential fully for them.

Openness has a sensorial "flavor," an experiential essence that you can learn to recognize if you look for it. If you want to be happy, practice that which lies at the root of all happiness: Engage and experience life, work, and people with all your being, instead of just with your thoughts and unconscious habits. As your joyfulness increases, so will your effectiveness. Although work may not be easy, joyfulness makes the entire process of work far more satisfying and sustainable.

What If Leadership Isn't Just About What You're Doing?

Despite everything I've told you thus far, do you still believe, as I once did, that making progress and being successful in business is solely or mainly about the actions you take?

And have you ever felt so much pain from not knowing what to do next that you were tempted to bring in an army of consultants to tell you? I am a coach, so I get a lot of inquiries from businesspeople who have realized they are in pain and don't know what to do about it. But although asking for advice and taking a variety of new actions seems reasonable on the surface, I assure you that the first step to freeing yourself from cycles of painful overwork and endless meetings and to-do lists is to look within. Hiring an expert to tell you how to fix your problems won't help if you are not also open internally. The real challenge when you're stuck, stressed, or confused about what to do is to address yourself on the level of your feelings. By allowing yourself to *not* know and just to be inquisitive and open, you can relieve the pressure.

The singular focus on action in our society is based on a fundamental flaw in thinking: the notion that "doing" is more important than the state of being of the "doer." We owe our obsession with action to the fact that little or no attention goes to asking "Who am I being?"

The belief *If I get what I want, then I will be happy* is fallacious thinking. In fact, if you are unhappy now and continue to be unhappy while you are working toward an accomplishment, you may well still be unhappy when you reach your goal. If your relationships were strained on the way to your destination, what could possibly make a lasting difference once you get there?

Even if you manage to patch up relationships that have frayed over the years, the goal you reach will only make you feel *relatively* better. Wouldn't you rather feel *absolutely* better all along?

Relative reality is the world of things. Absolute reality is the world of energy.

Having a positive inner state that remains undiminished no matter what type of external forces are brought to bear is possible if we don't source our identity in our results.

I Think, Therefore I Am **Not**

How does traditional Western thought teach us to overidentify with results? Because of our intense identification with our *thoughts.*

Hear me out.

A leading thinker of the Enlightenment, the 17th-century French mathematician and philosopher René Descartes, helped usher in a thought revolution that powered the engines of Western scientific, economic, and societal development when he wrote, *"Je pense, donc je suis"* ("I think, therefore I am"). Cartesian philosophy, and the impact of Enlightenment philosophers, continues to permeate Western culture. A core tenet of modern Western thought is anchored by the philosophy that we are entirely rational beings living in a rational world. In a way this infers that we are walking heads detached from bodies and feelings! It ignores the emotional drivers and experience of human behavior and the ways we relate with others. Western culture, influenced by Enlightenment philosophers, holds concepts that can be proven above those that can be experienced.

Although there were a number of positive impacts from the Enlightenment on the modern world, this particular view of human nature is far from enlightened.

Are leaders who are detached from their emotions perceived by others as trustworthy and credible? No, not usually. There has been much research on the power of emotional intelligence to build community, inspire loyalty, and increase engagement within organizations. Being able to recognize and imagine how others are feeling from reading their social cues begins with being able to sense how we ourselves are feeling and interpret our needs in the moment.

This steers us toward an initial discussion of using techniques borrowed from yoga to improve our approach to leadership. Yoga and other Eastern wisdom traditions recognize that the body is our most reliable compass in life. The body never lies. Becoming better acquainted with our bodies and the sensations we feel within them is the key to improving our human experience and making progress as leaders. The more we rely on our bodies to sense what is true for us, the more we disidentify with our thinking minds, which otherwise can trick us into maintaining old, self-limiting patterns of behavior. We can tell if the mind is feeding us a round of illusions.

Once we are in touch with the wisdom of the body, the thinking mind and its partner, that self-preserving, reactive aspect of our personalities known as the *ego,* can be relegated to their proper roles: They are useful for planning, organizing, managing, and acting. Although cognitive skills such as these are necessary to lead, none is sufficient to function as our leadership compass.

An overreliance on thought fails to take advantage of our full range of human capacities. One of these is the ability to connect openly with other people so that we genuinely perceive and respect their personhood and value their contributions rather than approaching them as objects that we can move around like pieces on a chessboard. Openness of connection to others is a cornerstone of overall leadership effectiveness.

The consequences of disconnection are devastating for leaders and those who work with them. Disconnecting from yourself and others is palpable and results in disintegration for individuals and organizations, which is reflected in high, sustained levels of stress. Leaders who are disconnected from themselves cannot help being disconnected from their employees *because it is only possible to lead from an internal perspective we have experienced.*

When we can't connect with or experience ourselves as we are in the present moment, we also can't hope to experience other people as they are. Rigidly focusing on objects and goals reflects a fixation on that which is outside us. And this derives from a fundamental misperception of where our efficacy as leaders is sourced.

Do you feel the need to micromanage your employees or team? Do you feel like people aren't listening to you? Do you feel distracted from your purpose? Turn your attention inward and make space for self-connection. Open your senses and awareness.

Being must precede *doing.* Leaders often say: "Help my people." They rarely say: "Help me learn how to *be* within myself so that I can truly connect to those with whom I work." But that is exactly what they need to do!

The Root of What Disconnects Us Lies Within Us

Managing our interior landscape is one of the most challenging human endeavors. It is the work of a lifetime and fundamental to improving leadership. So let me ask you: What do you imagine might happen if you shifted tactics and began using the energy you have been expending on making things happen and on maintaining a facade of invulnerability and control for *consciously managing yourself?* For self-regulating your inner state? This is the experiment in leadership I am encouraging you to initiate.

If you can resolve to drop your intense desire to know the answers and be perceived as an expert, go back to the beginning, and approach everything with the freshness of the first time, answers that have eluded you may suddenly appear. Or you may hear a quiet voice in the room you previously ignored.

Moreover, the dilemma we all face when shifting our attention to the state of our inner being is that it is natural to be motivated by our habitual thinking—fearful thoughts derived from pain in the past and anxious thoughts about scenarios that could occur in the future.

We like to think we will be happy when we attain our goals. That's one of the deceptions the egoic mind uses to tempt us to work on its agenda. It could be true, except for our tendency to repeat patterns of thought, feeling, and behavior. Customarily, when we arrive in the future, we are still unable to be present and happy because our attention turns to the next future. And the next. And the next after that.

We are in the bad habit of never experiencing our lives as we live them.

When we filter the present through memories or anticipation, we rob ourselves of living in the only time in which we can exist. Seen through a distorted lens of perception, life becomes an endless stream of moments in which we are not "here" and we can neither experience nor respond to what is actually happening.

We also cannot experience our own essence. Our energetic state.

Leaders are understandably reluctant to discount their hard-earned wisdom, gleaned from analyzing past successes and failures. They may believe that they are making integrated decisions based on the collected knowledge of a lifetime. They use their savvy to set up new goals and action plans, and in some cases, things work out well. However, if their experiences are heavily influenced by past fears or future anxieties, they are not applying true wisdom to their actions. In reality, they are just reliving the past again and again in the present.

As leaders, we must be able to adapt to the present and see new opportunities in it, as well as discern the differences between the past and present. We need to open our minds so we can perceive the moment.

As a survival mechanism, to save energy and enable us to react quickly to danger, the human brain evolved to learn from the past and anticipate the future. These predictive abilities can be helpful. We are often asked to make decisions based on incomplete information. In fact, waiting to get all the facts before you decide can immobilize teams and cause them to miss opportunities.

It's an efficient system. When we have to deal with incomplete information, we fill in the blanks. We are rewarded for our ability to make accurate inferences about the future. The trouble is that we believe we are conscious, rational decision-makers *all the time.*

Practicing being open to the present gets us better information, although still incomplete.

Let us also embrace the fact that our understanding of the information we do have access to will always be colored by a lifetime of subconscious programming that distorts our ability to be objective.

What does it look like in the real world when we try to solve problems based on habit or habitual thinking? Perhaps a leader has been promoted from within because they excelled in a number of functional areas. They may be used to leaning on identified strengths to solve problems. *I'm already good at these things, so why can't I keep doing them the same way in this new setting?* they may think. It is likely for them to become frustrated at some point because the habits that led to so many previous career successes no longer work well in their current role. In this situation, the leader is attached to seeing things through a filter from the past rather than being open to what is unfolding at present.

Most of us have come to identify ourselves with our professional goals at one point or another. We may believe that people are their ideas, habits, behaviors, profits, results, successes, and failures. If we esteem ourselves only because we've had positive results, we will want to do more of the same things. But chasing past results is like feeding a beast that can never be satiated. Eventually frustration will come. Those feelings of dissatisfaction all share the same source: that we are more than the sum of our thoughts and habits. More than our successes and failures. We need to be open to this realization as well.

Close-Mindedness Is Limiting and Stressful, Not Productive

Some leaders I've coached were initially unwilling to consider that their habits were acquired conditioning—and therefore could potentially be changed. For example, when asked how he thought he might create a healthier relationship with his workload, one client defensively responded, "My job is all or nothing. There is no part time. What am I supposed to do, quit?" He had become so emotionally attached to his habit of overworking that he believed there was no other way.

That's not to say that it's always easy or clear how to change a particular habit. Just that it's *possible* if change is your intention.

This fellow had become a victim of his own success. He had reached the painful point where he couldn't tolerate the relentless onslaught of tasks and problems to solve. His troubles at work were manifesting consequences in his personal life, and both his valued personal relationships and his health were being impaired. What was happening in his work, with his family, and in his heart, mind, and body were all related to the same inner conflict. Even so, he didn't believe or want to believe he had the power to change his habits.

You may be reluctant to change your hard-earned habits, too. What would make you want to?

These habits have worked for you in the past. They help your brain earn its operational efficiency. For example, when you first learned to drive a car (assuming you drive), it took an inordinate amount of brain processing capacity to operate the vehicle. Driving requires us to pay attention to so many things at once that even talking to a passenger can overwhelm a new driver. Yet after a few years, the act of driving becomes more habitual, does it not? This is because what once needed a lot of energy and attention now requires much less; your habit of driving has become efficient.

Why is this not an exclusively good thing? Because every habit, no matter how efficient, has a corresponding downside. Driving more efficiently is a positive until it causes people to multitask and have an accident. Just as some habits allow us to work less to perform a mundane task, others are designed to protect us from reexperiencing undigested emotional pain—pain that's carried in our subconscious mind and in every cell in our body. This is the trauma that determines how we treat ourselves and how we interact with the world. It infuses everything we think and do, and it is with us wherever we go.

Undigested fears and worries create unconscious behavioral habits that can impede or severely damage relationships. We may blame people when they don't share our internal reality. (From their perspective, it is shocking that we don't share theirs.) The truth is that each of us is living in our own reality. A mental conversation is going on inside our heads whenever we're awake, and this dialogue drives our behavior.

For example, we may be driven to overwork based on an underlying conversation about needing to bolster our worth or needing to be safe. This inner talk sounds like "I am not enough," "I am alone," and "I am unloved." Self-defensive belief structures mobilize an entire array of illogical thinking that causes us to become reactive rather than responsive. When memories, emotions, and thoughts from the past are triggered, they filter our view of the present and we become reactive.

A reactive mind prevents us from responding productively to the moment.

Any time we are reactive, because we are not effectively relating to ourselves in the moment, we cannot be present with others. Those who have been tasked with carrying out our objectives can sense our lack of clarity and misalignment. They may perceive us as "confused," for instance, and then our reactivity triggers their self-protective belief structures. Miscommunication becomes the norm when a reactive individual is leading a team. Other leaders and colleagues become disheartened and, ultimately, unproductive. Reactive leaders destroy their relationships unknowingly and unconsciously, not only at work, but also at home.

The truth of who we are is distorted by our ego-driven mental constructs. But there is hope for us because, in fact, *there is a self in each of us that has the capacity to observe all our identifications.*

Self-identification can be a false identity, such as "I am a hard worker," "I am superior because of my intellect," or "I am a failure." These selves are identified with experiences from our past, usually ones that caused us to feel afraid. We might work hard because at age 10, we were punished for receiving a low grade on a quiz and were frightened by losing the respect of our parents. These selves are also identified with our worries and expectations about the future.

These false identities are actually crowding out our ability to experience our one true self, which is the observer. You know the observer is genuine because it does not change over time or under varying conditions. The observer is the same whether we are young or old, rich or poor, male or female. It has no size, weight, or shape, no start or finish. It just is. And here's the catch: That true self can *only* be experienced in the present moment.

Our internal motivators, which push us to work and succeed, cause many of us to do things that destroy our bodies. We experience such stress from disconnection to our real self and suppressing our emotional pain that we may go to extreme lengths to quiet it. If this becomes too intense or lasts a long time, we may reach for a way to self-soothe, including various addictions: overwork, food, alcohol, drugs, gambling, shopping, or sex, among other things.

That's Just How It Is—Or Is It?

Habits also affect how receptive leaders are to their colleagues and employees. Consider a colleague who comes to meetings and only offers negative feedback, saying things like, "This will never work. That can't be done. We've never done it that way before. We don't have what it takes to do that." It's understandable that you would expect this pattern to continue. But if you are only able to see them as a walking ball of negativity, based on your past experiences, you might miss out on a good idea they have to contribute.

Your colleague's negativity is not only self-destructive; it is also destructive to the organization and the morale of their co-workers. But your own disconnection from the truth of the moment is also destructive. By prejudging a colleague, you are missing out on the opportunity to positively interact with them or influence their behavior, and both of these things matter.

A healthy yet skeptical outlook is helpful. Would you want a contract written by your lawyer that only foresaw favorable outcomes? The invitation is to transform negativity into a healthy dynamic so that co-creativity and joy are both possible. You need to be open to the possibilities that each of us possess.

When You Are Open, the Answers Reveal Themselves to You

To influence others positively, you must be able to inspire them. But to do that, you must first be able to inspire yourself. The word *inspire* comes from the Latin words *in + spirare* ("to breathe"). Inspiration is the result of connecting to your own spirit—your true self—which functions like an inner compass. You will know when you have opened this connection because you will *feel* it, and a flow of insights will commence. And, like a river that draws water from the mountains and empties to the sea, the flow is ever renewable.

Once you begin opening to your true self and following its guidance, you will notice, *Things are happening so much more easily now. I'm getting better results with less effort. Solutions are appearing organically.* With regular practice, much of the stress of working drops away, and interactions with everyone in and around your business—staff, colleagues, vendors, customers, and clients—become more open and less limited, too. Conflict lessens.

Self-influence is the only kind of influence that is sustainable. And it is completely under your control.

Your Real Circle of Influence

To influence another person requires knowing where your true power lies: in the ability to avoid identifying with your fears and habits. If your internal dialogue is conflicted, your actions may also be in conflict with your intentions, and you are likely to create conflict with others. To truly accept other people as they are requires radical self-acceptance. When this is available to you, you will be able to access your innate ability to co-create with other people.

Co-creative communication is not about "What can you do for me?" or "What can I get from you?" When you use your influence appropriately, communication shifts to "How can *we* move forward based on our mutual goals?" and you focus on validating the creativity of everybody involved.

I invite you to dial into perceiving people's abilities *at this moment*, regardless of what has happened in the past or your worries about what might happen in the future. This ability to be present with yourself and then connect to others is the gateway for successful collaboration.

In an open state of being, when your mind is clear and free of conflict, the solutions that emerge will be bigger than any you could have achieved with demands or force. You are now leading through love. And love is the greatest leader.

Open to the One Who Is Observing

We've established the flaw of believing that we are our thoughts. Yet we all have encountered people clinging desperately to their beliefs as if their thoughts have built concrete watchtowers from whose heights they defend their perspective from the world.

Openness refers to an entirely different experience, an experience of being the *observer of your thoughts*. Thoughts come and go in your mind, like clouds floating by in a vast, open sky. They have only the power you choose to give them. The self-protective ego would have you abdicate your sovereignty to it. But there are ways to respond to its urgings in a healthy manner.

Shortly, I will show you how to observe your thoughts and emotions from a distance, as a witness. Learning this skill opens the door to the present moment—and to the infinite possibilities you can create when you are present in the now.

Cultivate Openheartedness

The brain is a powerful organ that excels at codifying, organizing, labeling, and interpreting. Yet it needs to work in tandem with other powerful organs, such as the gut and the heart. When we open ourselves to experiencing the moment in an integrated manner—with head, heart, and energy aligned—we discover that the heart and sensations from other parts of our bodies can also lead us. This can be difficult for leaders who believe that openheartedness and vulnerability are weaknesses. Yet that is *exactly* what we need to cultivate.

One of my coaching clients, Vince, opened his mind and heart to find a winning solution for a botched customer scenario that had been building for more than a year. Internal problems with his company's processes and systems, combined with the same or worse on the part of his customer's company, had created a perfect storm. It was Vince's job to resolve the mess and obtain a settlement to which both sides could agree.

I asked Vince, "What do you think the VP with whom you'll be meeting will be entering the room believing and feeling?" He was able to imagine what it would be like for this individual—all the pressure he was feeling—and how provoked he might be as a result of the history between their companies.

Next, I asked him, "What can you control about all of this?"

He responded, "I can control how I am when I enter the room." Yes!

Before the meeting, Vince practiced centering himself and getting present to this imaginary negotiation, and then speaking as an open, receptive leader.

On our next call, he couldn't wait to tell me how well things had gone. "Not only did we get more money in resolution than we had anticipated," he said, "but we also talked about how we were going to work together again in the future!"

Vince credited his ability to open himself first as the essential ingredient that changed the outcome from "lose-lose" for the past year to "win-win" for his company and for its customer.

Have a Beginner's Mind

To go from living reactively to living responsively requires being receptive to an entirely different experience. Zen Buddhism refers to this as *shoshin* ("beginner's mind" in Japanese). It refers to letting go of the filters of perception so that you can experience things as they are now without prejudice. How you experience the sensations in your body *precedes* the ability to engage in action. That action is thus informed and changed by the present-moment experience.

Where do these distortions of the present moment live within us? How do we let go of our past fears and future anxieties in order to be present? How do we access them so we can change our relationship with them? What do we need to do differently to let them go? How do we get to *shoshin*? How do we experience the present moment in our bodies through our energy?

In yoga, we call the feeling of energy in our bodies *prana*. But this energy is universal, found all around us as well as within us. The present moment lives in a body, with mind, heart, and being responding harmoniously together.

How can we be energetically connected to those around us when we're not energetically connected to ourselves? When we are living as who we are not, we are leading from who we are not. We are distorting our connection to others. When we destroy ourselves and our relationships to achieve a goal, we destroy our ability to enjoy the journey of life, and the goals we achieve after gutting ourselves to achieve them can never produce the happiness we seek.

To attain the best version of ourselves, we have to recognize that when we allow our subconscious programs—our conditioning—to control us, we limit access to who we really are. Therefore, be open to discovering that you are not simply the sum of your thoughts, beliefs, habits, and accomplishments. You are much, much more.

Leaders must become aware that the conflict they feel within themselves has roots in their internal perceptions. Without changing those perceptions, they will continually create conflict and stress with others. Looking inside ourselves through the lens of a curious observer is fundamental to improving our leadership effectiveness.

A 2016 *Harvard Business Review* research study looked at three specific areas of self-mastery that allow leaders to be more present and thoughtful: *metacognition,* the ability to step back and observe at a distance what is happening around you; *allowing,* or being open to what is happening without judging yourself or others; and *curiosity.*[2] The most effective leaders were those who committed to a level of practice, at least 10 minutes every day. These individuals had a strong sense of curiosity and were open to learning more about all situations.

Also remember: Only you can change yourself. No one else has the power to change you. Moreover, your external reality reflects your internal world—the world of your thoughts, beliefs, and emotions. These determine how you act, engage, and lead. To address your internal way of seeing yourself is to take the first step to impact that which is outside you.

Opening Practices

Try the following two practices for opening your awareness and your heart:

EXERCISE 1: **Opening Your Awareness**

Whenever you feel constricted or out of options, or when you just want to feel open and present, you can expand your awareness with this easy process, which takes only two or three minutes to do. This seated exercise is an excellent refocusing technique for transitioning between activities.

1. Sit on a stable chair, with your "sit bones" almost all the way to the front edge. Rest your hands comfortably on your thighs or let them hang passively by your sides. Your eyes may be open or closed.

2. Lengthen and straighten your spine. Imagine you are stacking your vertebrae one atop the other, like dishes in a kitchen cabinet.

3. Pull your shoulders up to your ears a few times before relaxing them naturally—and feel your neck lengthening each time you release them.

4. Make your chin parallel to the floor.

5. Feel your feet grounding into the floor.

6. Now place one hand on your belly and the other on your chest and slowly breathe in through your nose with your mouth closed, expanding your belly, rib cage, and chest, in that order, until the air reaches the top of your lungs.

7. Hold your breath for three or four seconds, without straining.

EXERCISE 1: **Opening Your Awareness, cont.**

8. Release your breath gradually in the reverse order, emptying the top of your lungs and then allowing the breath to travel down through your rib cage and abdomen before exhalation.

9. Repeat the same breathing pattern for three to five cycles of breathing in and out.

10. Replace your hands on your thighs or by your sides and breathe normally. Notice what you are aware of now that you were not aware of before.

EXERCISE 2: **Opening Your Heart**

You'll need to get down on the floor to do this exercise, which requires a couple of props. I suggest that you read through the instructions before you execute the steps.

1. Lie down on your back on the floor. Place a foam roller or padded yoga bolster horizontally behind the lower edge of your shoulder blades. If you don't have either of these, place a pillow under your upper back so that your sternum (breastbone) can easily but gently stretch open. To avoid straining your neck, you may lay one or more folded yoga blankets or towels or a second pillow behind your head. There should be no pain involved. Modifications: If the suggested position feels too extreme, you may lower the height of the object you're lying on. A folded towel or blanket may be substituted. Also feel free to place a pillow under your knees or bend your knees to relieve any strain on your lower back.

2. Settle into a relaxed position, breathing regularly, opening your arms out wide to the sides of your body. Feel your chest and sternum opening up.

3. Inhale through your nose, pulling air into your body and gently expanding your torso.

4. Imagine the breath going to your heart, where it is opening, softening, and whispering to the area and energy all around your heart.

5. Release the breath from your heart, allowing your belly to flatten as you exhale.

6. Stay and breathe in this position as long as you enjoy it!

EXERCISE 2: **Opening Your Heart, cont.**

7. To end the stretch, roll over to one side with your knees bent and rest there for a few moments.

8. Place your hands on the floor and push yourself up.

9. Check in with yourself. What emotions did you feel as your heart opened? What is different for you after doing this exercise?

CHAPTER 2

Learn

Reorient Your Focus

*Leaders are more powerful role models when
they learn than when they teach.*[1]

—ROSABETH MOSS KANTER

As a leader, over the years you will have acquired a vast array of skills and built a library of resources to draw on as needed. Among these are habits of thought you've developed (based on experience) that you believe make you more effective. You may also be a regular consumer of products teaching "success habits" (like this very book), which are popular for the obvious reason that businesspeople are playing a high-stakes game and we all want to be competent and do the "right" things to save time, energy, and effort. But despite every tool already in your toolkit, you could get stuck or feel lost when faced with a new challenge.

Because conditions in business are constantly changing, occasional bafflement is to be expected. Many leaders find their hard-won skills insufficient to address important problems.

Do you and members of your leadership team have trouble adapting to rapid change? As your organization grows and your sphere of influence increases, is it becoming more difficult for you to influence the people you need to help you achieve a vision or goal? Then life may be inviting—or demanding!—you to learn something new about how to regulate your energy and attention.

The fundamental flaw in most leadership development models is that they rely on formulas that are based on incorrect knowledge. These approaches ask us to focus primarily on problem solving and action taking, with rarely a mention of our state of being. Yet the latter is where a leader's efforts often fall apart. *The point at which leaders stop being able to develop and grow is the point at which their organizations stop growing as well.*

In the last chapter, we explored the concept of opening ourselves to something beyond our unconscious habits. Openness is a prerequisite for learning that carries us beyond the known and into the realm of being and feeling and presence. In this chapter, I will guide you to reorient your focus by introducing you to the five hallmarks of *being-based leadership.*

Reorientation of Your Focus Is Necessary

The 24/7 nature of a digitally connected global system hijacks our physiology and puts us into a permanent fight-or-flight mode. Although our modern work world has no saber-toothed tigers we need to outrun, our nervous systems react as if we are constantly being chased by them.

We have two counterbalancing components to our nervous system, the sympathetic and the parasympathetic. The sympathetic mode prepares us for short bursts of intense activity, such as saving ourselves from a predator or a natural cataclysm. The parasympathetic mode is for relaxation and access to our higher intelligence, including creativity. It also helps our digestion function effectively, so the body can create energy. Some people call this the rest-and-digest mode.

We were not designed to live in one or the other mode. We were built to alternate between extremes and stay largely in the middle of the range. Our health, vitality, and joy depend on learning to experience ourselves always in balance.

Too many of us are living in *duality*, a state of imbalance in which the sympathetic nervous system seems always to be on high alert. This sympathetic state was designed to be used for short periods of activity, followed by a time of recovery. Living in one extreme of our nervous system causes great stress on our body and mind.

Mentally, duality is characterized by all-or-none, black-and-white thinking. "It's us vs. them" or "me vs. you." "It's my way or the highway." It leads to prejudice and mistrust, competition for resources, division, and fear. At its worst, it's close-minded, paranoid, and conflict-ridden.

When the burden of living in sympathetic overdrive becomes too heavy, we stoke ourselves with coffee and other stimulants to maintain our state of high alert. As our bodies and psyches endure physical and emotional pain from living out of harmony, we will do anything to soothe our self-inflicted misery—including addiction to alcohol, drugs, or gambling, among other things. We do all this to essentially "vacate" our painful bodies and minds, and we often succeed in being absent or partially absent. And when we are not present within ourselves, our relationships become strained or even damaged. Others sense this and believe us to be untrustworthy.

How can we be present with others when we are not even present within ourselves? If we do not accept ourselves, how can we accept others? How can we co-create positive outcomes when we can't create a safe and productive relationship with others?

The natural balance between the sympathetic and parasympathetic states is where you can find calm and inner peace. This is the state of *polarity,* where opposites are in balance. When we are in polarity—a dynamically balancing state of being—our bodies naturally heal from stress and injury, as they were designed to do. Our emotional states also become balanced, and our relationships can improve. We are resilient and feel whole. This ability to consciously choose to stay in a balanced state is a prerequisite for maintaining personal power, staying grounded, and establishing trust with others.

Mentally, polarity is characterized by thoughts about checking in and seeing if there is anything we need as far as self-care. The inner switch techniques help us be dynamic and pull ourselves back from the edge of the cliff—or take flight from it on wings!

The difference between the deadlock of duality and the dynamism of polarity raises another important set of questions. Why would we voluntarily destroy our inner peace and joy? What goal could possibly be worth throwing our health and well-being out the window? What would make us choose to live in duality instead of polarity? How have we come to neglect our birthright?

Without a doubt, we make these insane choices because we don't know any better. We do it to avoid experiencing ourselves as who we are instead of who we are not. We do it to avoid experiencing our own energy as we are meant to live.

Of course, we don't voluntarily do any of these things. We do them subconsciously.

Living in duality is the flaw of the Cartesian thinking that informs much of our culture, which believes that we are (or ought to be) rational, and that emotions are somehow separate.

We may also be driven by our past experiences, which filter this moment through the lens of our fears and anxieties. We are therefore almost always living through our past experiences or focused on future goals, even when we think we are living in the moment. When the future finally arrives, we are already looking for that "next great thing."

Leaders can rationalize their overdrive by saying they have to do certain things to create the future. However, when that future arrives, the leader will not be present, just as they are not present now. Therefore, we are held captive in a self-imposed prison in the past or future by the subconscious. All we see is the darkness of our past pain filtered through preconditioned experiences. We never experience the lightness of life that can only be felt in the present.

This is why you must reorient your focus.

Learning May Be More Than You Think It Is

Most people think of learning as acquiring knowledge or a technical or functional skill. And, yes, cultivating new skills may be required to advance in your career. For instance, you might need to learn Spanish or Japanese or study accounting and the tax code. However, as your responsibilities increase, technical skills and information may be insufficient to lead.

Leaders actually need to learn something entirely different, which is how to go beyond the limitations of their minds—beyond their conditioning and experience.

The type of leadership we are exploring in this book is initiated in the body. Traditional leadership training focuses on "what to think about" and "how to speak to others." Rarely does it address "how to be." But "being" has greater potential, and the body is the gateway to being.

When coaching leaders, I frequently ask, "Who do you need to *be* to make this or that happen?" They often respond, "What do you mean—*be*?" It's as if there is a wall inside them separating the "be-er" from the "do-er!" When self-assessing, it doesn't initially occur to some leaders to include who they really are underneath the role they're playing as the leader of their organization, department, or team.

Although the body could not be more present in our lives—in fact, it is inescapable, even when we are numb to its sensations or ignore its signals—as leaders we are taught by society and business convention to override its needs.

As long as we are on the fool's errand of trying to achieve happiness through our "doing" rather than our "being," we may achieve success at our task, but fail to feel happiness. If we are oriented exclusively to action aimed at achieving success, the best we can ever hope for is to feel *relatively* happier than before we reached our goal. However, there is no achievement that will make us absolutely happy permanently.

The persistent and absolute happiness we seek is only possible if we are oriented to the eternal ground of our being, the true self that is connected to everything that exists on the level of energy. Given this, why not begin by emphasizing our being? Why not start from the position of feeling joyous throughout the journey regardless of its outcome, encompassing successes and failures, ups and downs, industry disruptions, and exciting opportunities?

And what if we resolve to measure our success as leaders and our worth as human beings by who we are in every moment, not just by if we are getting where we want to go? Then our experience of happiness is independent of the outcomes we achieve.

If our objective then is to move from a state of *thinking and doing* to a state of *feeling and being,* the knowledge we need has to come from a tradition that shares this value, which is why we are turning to the inward-oriented practices of yoga, not all of which take place on a mat.

Many people who do yoga or meditation feel their practice helps them maintain their equanimity and inner peace. Sometimes they even briefly feel free from struggle and suffering. However, from time to time they find that they still get "stuck." They may find that any improvement is only temporary before they yo-yo back to their initial state. The gains are not sustainable. Why is that?

What is missing is the *integration of good knowledge with good practices.* Either one by itself is insufficient to maintain us in the state of feeling and being. We may revert to thinking and doing exclusively—or, even worse, to dissociating completely.

Sometimes when you are in a conversation with someone, you can feel that they aren't "there." Whether they're looking away, agitated, or even hyperventilating, they're not tracking with you. When this happens, that person is dissociated from their presence. They are living in a different moment than now and out of touch with the condition of their body.

Imagine we are planning a cross-country road trip from New York to California. If we just get on a highway and drive without knowing which direction we are heading, it is unlikely we will reach our destination. Without a map, we will lose our way.

Knowing where to direct your energy and attention is a critical component of leadership. This knowledge will give you an inner roadmap to guide you from who you are currently to becoming who you need to be to reach your goals.

You will need to establish practices that maintain your well-being. Examples of these may include yoga, breath work, tai chi, sleeping well, eating a healthy diet, and exercising regularly, as well as nourishing your inner being mentally, emotionally, and spiritually.

Accountability Is Key to Successful Learning

It may help to have an accountability partner to maintain consistency in your well-being practices, as starting a new set of habits can be daunting. A study by the American Society for Training and Development showed that the probability of reaching your goal goes from 10 percent if you simply have an idea to 95 percent if you have made a commitment and a specific appointment to share the commitment with an accountability partner.[2] Developing a new habit takes on average 66 days of repeating a new behavior, according to a 2009 study published in the *European Journal of Social Psychology*. During this initial period of integration, having an accountability process in place helps to facilitate and embed the learning.

Without human connection—that is, without someone demonstrating that they care about your vision and your progress—efforts to reliably change your behavior are likely to fail. As the leader of an organization, you must take responsibility for asking for the accountability you need from a trusted individual. You also have a responsibility to provide this same support to the people who report to you.

It's understandable that leaders feel disheartened about promises that things can change—they usually don't. If you hope to create an effective development program in your company, you will need to meet your people where they are and co-create with them the outcomes, goals, and behaviors necessary to achieve the results you and they want. Modeling feeling and being yourself is an important step in shifting organizational culture.

When I am coaching inside organizations, I take people through a sequential learning and behavioral change process that supports them in adopting new behaviors in baby steps. In time, these small steps create habits and larger changes that are effective and sustainable. When you create wellness or human development programs, break them down into small units of change, and then monitor progress and challenges along the way. Build in accountability for every step.

The Five Hallmarks of Being-Based Leadership

Some leaders think they will "be" someone when they achieve a certain goal—a promotion, additional compensation, or some other desired status. They think they will be happy when they finally obtain or achieve what they want. Many will "practice being unhappy" until they reach the goal, not realizing that being unhappy all along the way toward their promised happiness only creates a pattern of unhappiness. Think about it: How will you achieve your way into happiness if you have been miserable the entire way there?

Others think that the path to happiness, as with the Velveteen Rabbit, lies in "becoming": when you've received so much love that your fur is worn thin. But the model of *becoming* implies that there is something missing at the outset of our journey. Anything we believe we are lacking makes us unhappy because we are attached to our goals more than to our being. If we can become aware of our being and focus on that instead, we can be happy all along the way toward the goal. This simple shift in perspective changes everything.

What truly matters is how we are on the journey of getting where we want to go.

There are five hallmarks by which we can recognize ourselves and others as being-based leaders. Do you embody this paradigm? Where might you want to modify your current approach?

Hallmark 1: Self-Inquiring

For being-based leaders, *being always precedes doing*. Knowing that the actions available to them are informed by their inner state, the leaders engage in regular self-inquiry.

Many leaders believe that their state of being is determined by a mixture of genetics, the environment, and the effects of their experiences. Some believe that "people either have it or they don't." They think leaders who spend time processing their emotions are ineffective and slow and will lose to their competitors through some sort of "survival of the fittest." They view feeling and being as soft skills that don't merit the investment of any resources.

These doing-oriented leaders want efficient, low-maintenance people for their organizations. They believe that people come to work with brains that are somehow disconnected from their feelings. This way of thinking can cause them to view employees and colleagues—and even themselves—as objects whose sole purpose is to complete desired tasks.

But how could anyone who is treated like a machine manifest creativity, much less innovate with others?

Though many people believe our personality traits and behaviors are hard-wired and therefore difficult to modify, being-based leaders understand and adjust their behavior through self-examination. They take time to ruminate on open-ended questions like: *Is it possible that our state of being can be chosen and is not intrinsic to our personality? Can we modify a state of being or a habit just by becoming aware of it? Do we need intention? Practice? Anything else?*

Before you can modify a state of being, you need to recognize that it exists. You need to be willing to look objectively at yourself and feel your emotions until you establish a foundation of knowledge about yourself. Self-exploration is a process that cannot be completed overnight.

We often make decisions automatically, out of habit, which is not ideal. In an unconscious state, we lose the ability to respond appropriately to what is taking place in the moment we are in *right now* and instead rely on a pattern of behavior that we developed to cope with a challenge in the past. As long as we continue to hold this pattern in our body and mind, we inadvertently rely on our reactive "habits."

What happens when we make a choice by acting from an unconscious state of fear or anxiety? When we lead from this state of fear, anxiety, and ego, in reality, *we are being led.* Our unconscious habits are leading us. When we are living in a reactive state, we are detached from our body, relying instead on the reactive habit to cope.

Our bodies are designed to integrate massive amounts of information and process it with ease. However, when we are in an unconscious state, we lose the ability to integrate or access this important somatic information. We cannot function in the ways we are meant to function when we are living in an unconscious, reactive pattern derived from the past when we were in crisis or afraid for our life.

Until we learn how to shift out of our fear-based patterns and create a conscious way of being, we cannot solve problems effectively, either on our own or with others. All we get is a magnified manifestation of our preconditioned fears and anxieties. This creates what we may consider as a *blowup.*

Wouldn't you rather allow your inner leader to be out front? When you repair the separation from your true self, you will understand that the solution you have sought from others can only happen when you first solve the problem within yourself and go from being unconscious and distracted to being conscious and present.

Hallmark 2: Consciousness and Presence

It is not surprising that leaders feel their hard-won habits and wisdom make them perfectly suited to take on new challenges. These things often bring them professional success, acclaim, and financial reward, confirming that they played by the rules and "won." But they're working so hard that they're missing out on the joy of living. In the process, have they won by creating suffering for themselves and others along the way?

There is a survival advantage in relying on learning from the past. It is much more efficient for our brains to establish habits, so that we don't use up our capacity for cognitive processing each day on repetitive activities such as driving or washing dishes. But if we aren't careful, our minds can trick us into making snap judgments about people and situations based on what has happened in the past—and these expectations may prove to be wrong, interfere with social bonding, or block innovation.

To some degree, all of us rely on knowledge we have acquired. As we discussed in Chapter 1, "Open," the trouble is that this knowledge is filtered through an unconscious lens, colored by fears from the past or anxieties about the future. These lenses distort our view of the present and therefore prevent us from "seeing things as they are." What we see is an illusion—we see it through the rearview mirror of our past conditioning. When we do this, we limit ourselves, and we limit the potential to find new solutions to pressing problems. What is novel in the present becomes reimagined as a distorted image of the past.

When something new triggers emotions similar to those we have already experienced, the brain sorts through its file drawers, searching for a response to that emotion that we used in the past. However, the hurt that the reactive mind was protecting us from isn't happening right now. We relive the protection of the hurt every time it is triggered, obscuring or even distorting the present moment as it is. In this way, although our habits save brain energy, they also prevent us from being present to novel experiences. This stops us from being able to adapt appropriately to change.

Furthermore, if past fears or future worries were programmed into us as suffering, then the present circumstances will stimulate those suffering neurons to fire up. Any action taken through this lens of past suffering will destroy your opportunity to create a different outcome—one that is more suitable to this moment. By dragging baggage from the past into the present, we can't travel lightly to our new destinations! Unless we understand this clearly, we will always be at risk of getting dragged into the past, reacting to stimuli that remind us of similar situations. We become prisoners of the past rather than unfettered beings who respond to the needs of the present.

There are other subconscious ways in which we introduce bias into our ways of perceiving the now. These include cultural, gender, religious, generational, and tribal, among other societal influences. We learn these preferences early in our lives, so they become "transparent" to us. They are so thoroughly installed into our subconscious thinking patterns that we don't even consider them biases or filters. We perceive them as true and cannot imagine that others do not share our perspective.

These patterns give us a sense of our place in the world as we grow up. We appreciate them for the grounding and connection they offer. However, our cultural discourse, although "true" for us, is not shared by everyone else. It is important that we be aware of how these influences have shaped our thinking and develop the ability to consciously choose when to engage them in present moment conversations with others. When we are fully conscious and aware, we can decide to move in a direction that is generative rather than repetitive.

Hallmark 3: Awareness of Your Own Energy

The third hallmark is to become aware of your own energy, a vital step toward feeling your way into being. There are words for energy in many Eastern languages. In Sanskrit, it is called *prana*. In Mandarin Chinese, it is called *chi*. In the West, our understanding of energy is more rudimentary.

We associate the word with either high or low states of being. We are awake or asleep, excited or tired, present or spaced out—many of our problems with energy stem from our determination to increase it artificially. We seek outside stimulants, such as coffee, cigarettes, or pills. Our need to overwork depletes us further, exacerbating our already depleted stores of energy.

From an ancient yogic perspective, our ability to experience and manage our energetic states is already hard-wired within us. In Sanskrit, energetic points are referred to as *chakras*. Similar energetic markers are described in a number of Eastern and Western traditions.[3]

Western concepts of energy belie the importance of our energetic internal system as a guidepost for activity in the world. I've observed time and again that communication, influence, inspiration, and overall effectiveness depend on understanding and activating our innate energetic resources.

We lack both good knowledge and good practices to access and live in our pure energetic natural state. Our energetic state of being, either awake or asleep, is the most rudimentary of our physical states. Our energetic state is naturally designed to be balanced and *balancing*—in other words, in polarity.

What type of energy are you sharing? Leaders work with and through others. If leaders are aware of their own energy, they can use it to positively influence a conversation. Conversely, if they are unaware of their own energy and its importance, they can potentially spread negative energy to others, hindering their ability to be effective or even having a damaging effect on them. In addition to encouraging ineffectiveness, it invites resistance. It can create a toxic work environment. *Energy, good or bad, is contagious.*

Positive energy enhances. Negative energy destroys. Any activity for which you feel a lack of energy is bound to seem burdensome and is likely to result in a less than positive outcome. Fortunately, when we connect to our own natural energy, it's often enough to effectively power any external endeavor.

Exercise to Experience Your Prana

Here is a simple exercise to tangibly feel your innate life force.

EXERCISE 3: **Experience Your Prana**

1. Rub your hands together until you feel some heat.

2. Keeping your palms pressed together, gently close your eyes and inhale deeply, down into your abdomen. Then exhale slowly and purposefully.

3. Slowly move your hands to shoulder width apart, palms still facing each other.

4. Slowly bring the palms toward each other until you feel a sense of pressure, as if there is a ball in between your hands. This is your prana, or energy field.

5. Move your hands in and out to shape the ball while feeling it expand and contract as you do, while continuing to breathe as in Step 2, exhaling slowly and purposefully.

6. Enjoy sensing and experiencing your own energy!

Hallmark 4: Intrinsic Connections Between the Physical Body and the Mind

According to Ayurveda, a sister science of yoga and the traditional medicine system of India that includes dietary and lifestyle practices, our bodies are highly intelligent machines that are designed to maintain homeostasis in the right conditions. This includes a healthy lifestyle based on the harmony found within the natural cycles of the earth and body-appropriate nutrition and exercise. When we manage ourselves in such a way, the autonomic mechanisms of balance in our bodies work entirely in the background without effort. We can best enjoy the delights of our bodies in these conditions. We can also use our mind-body connection best when our bodies and lifestyles are in balance.

When we eat too much or consume food that lacks nutritional value, our bodies cannot digest this food properly. The undigested food turns into excess fat and toxins, two sources of inflammation and disease. Healing requires knowledge, discipline, and effort. Losing unhealthy weight may take a long time and requires that we create a different relationship to food and our emotions around eating. When we diet, we are using the excess food energy that was stored in the body previously. Frequently, weight that is lost is later regained. We may think that our excess weight and disease are "who we are." We may even use medications to alleviate the symptoms without correcting the underlying problems. Sometimes the medical treatments have side effects or complications, thereby compounding the initial problem.

Similarly, "undigested" emotions and traumatic memories can not only be harmful at the time they are experienced, but also later—because they are stored in our minds as well as in our bodies and energy. Traumatic experiences stored in our bodies, just like food, represent the consequences of undigested emotions from the time of occurrence. We may use medications or even nonprescription drugs or alcohol to soothe our distress. These methods can likewise lead to secondary problems of their own.

Finally, we can create conflict and trauma within ourselves, which also gets stored in our bodies. When we do not take responsibility for our self-generated inner conflict, we maintain internal trauma that likewise cannot be digested. No amount of arguing, controlling, or blaming others can heal a conflict that starts inside us.

The conflicts we generate at work with our co-workers frequently manifest at home as well, during our interactions with our partners, spouses, or children. We create conflict within our social groups, religious communities, or any other group with whom we affiliate. Our conflicts show up in any situation in which we find ourselves. In the words of mindfulness-based stress-reduction expert Jon Kabat-Zinn, "Wherever you go, there you are."[4]

The many conflicts we feel manifest in our bodies, our minds, and our energy. We habitually try to mask the chatter in our heads in a variety of ways. We can mask our repetitive thoughts with overwork or other forms of self-soothing, as described previously. We can try to understand our minds better with therapy or by reading self-help books. We can even practice radical forgiveness in the hope that we can let go of some of our psychic pain. But why does the chatter of our monkey mind persist? Why do the repetitive thoughts, past fears, and future anxieties continue to circle within us like a vortex? Why do our pain and suffering keep coming back to haunt us?

In our Western paradigm, we primarily focus on fixing the mind *or* the body. Our medical model considers them separate and unrelated entities, but the problems created by the mind cannot be fixed by the mind alone. Instead, we need to integrate knowledge of the body. The body is all-knowing. It never lies.

Traumatic imprints that have become embedded within the mind, heart, and body cannot be removed through interventions that focus only on the mind. When you have conflict within your body, it spills over into all your actions and behaviors. Would we ever wash just one sock in the pair and expect our feet to feel clean? Any "healing" you do in your mind will be incomplete. The body will revert to whatever is held there. Is it any wonder that so many New Year's resolutions, made only with our minds, are broken in a matter of weeks? Likewise, our unresolved fears and anxieties that are stored in every cell in our bodies will filter the present through those lenses with the slightest provocation. "Fight, flight, or freeze" is more than just an experience of the mind—it involves every cell, nerve, and organ in our bodies.

We often think of our bodies as largely working automatically—carrying out breathing, digestion, and elimination, all beneath the level of our subconscious thinking mind. However, the field of yoga has taught us that through the conscious use of breath, we can access the autonomic aspects of our bodies.

We all know that breath patterns that originate from the top of our lungs create anxiety and that slow, methodical breathing that originates in the abdomen can induce calm. Although times have changed and there are many new breathing techniques for childbirth, many expectant mothers are taught Lamaze breathing because it can reduce pain.

Just as conscious breath control can be used to moderate the physical pain of childbirth, it can similarly be used to moderate psychic pain. The integration of mind and body occurs through the gateway of the breath. When we are experiencing fear or anxiety, we can hyperventilate or breathe excessively, causing low levels of carbon dioxide in the blood that can make you feel faint, dizzy, or light-headed. Slow, deep breathing helps your body transition from a sympathetically activated state to one that is in balance with the parasympathetic system. This will be covered in more detail in Chapter 4, "Drop In."

To change the patterns that hold the fears and anxieties within both our minds and bodies, we can reset our entire being simply by changing our breath. By consciously controlling our breath, we can control the state of our mind and body, including those elements that are outside of the scope of conscious awareness.

If our bodies are imbalanced, our capacity to integrate through our breath is diminished. This is where giving our bodies what they need to be healthy becomes critical. Healthy food, quality sleep, exercise, weight management, detoxification, and stress reduction, among others, are requisite pillars for leaders who desire to be truly balanced. How can we effectively lead if we don't value our bodies and what they need for well-being?

But even if our bodies are out of balance or we are ill, we can still use breath practices to move toward our body's natural state of homeostasis and wellness. In time, we will enhance our practices to include well-being. It's a circle with many points along the way. You can start wherever you are and move around the circle of wellness until you have filled in all the missing gaps between the points. Yoga is more than the physical postures. It offers a comprehensive system of well-being, including physical, mental, and emotional aspects, as well as dietary and lifestyle considerations.

Knowledge without practice is not effective, and practice without knowledge is also ineffective. We cannot think our way into deconstructing problems created by the mind, nor can we stretch our way into enlightenment! Only with good knowledge *and* good practice can we become truly integrated, present, fully alive beings.

Hallmark 5: Being the Witness

Developing a clear mind—one that is present and, therefore, unbiased from the experiences of the past—is key. But how?

As we have discussed, subconscious programming and our embodied underlying conversations create a running monkey mind filled with past fears and future anxieties. In this state, our interpretation of the present is distorted when we assign our memories the same relevance as what is happening now. But the mental, subconscious, and embodied memories in and of themselves are meaningless. They gain power over us when we act on our memories rather than on what is happening now. This stifles our creativity, as we are prevented from seeing possible solutions in the present, were we not being held back by our attachment to the past.

These memory-based filters take us from the present to a past event that resembles some aspect of the present. We interpret the present as being a repetition of the past because of subconscious past programming. The underlying programs—based on fears and anxieties—can be activated in a millisecond. The triggers can prompt us to react in surprising ways. Our triggers are similar to a hologram—with a hologram, any piece contains the entire three-dimensional structure of the hologram. Likewise, any single component of our past traumas can trigger the entire trauma. Therefore, a seemingly unrelated event with a single component that resembles a past trauma can cause us to dissociate in the present.

When we are shaped in this way, our capacity to create something positive is not available. Not only do we lose opportunities, but we also suffer in the process. Let me illustrate with a real-life example from a CEO who had become frustrated with people in her organization who did not assess the risks associated with the COVID-19 pandemic in the same way she did. Marianne had assimilated the latest knowledge from science and public health sources. She understood many of the disruptive risks of the pandemic to her employees and clients, and to her and their business activities. She assumed that her employees would respond rationally to data, logic, and her plan to handle the situation. What she got instead was a lot of pushback based on fear and emotion that didn't make sense to her. The more she tried to explain her plan and persuade them to support it, the more entrenched they became in their positions and the more they rambled on about the same fears.

Weeks went by, and Marianne thought she was communicating she had heard them, but she couldn't understand why all their conversations still felt circular. No progress was being made. She knew she was wasting valuable time that was needed to handle pressing business issues. She was now suffering—she felt triggered, in conflict, and ineffective. She was confused and frustrated and could not see a way to navigate out of the stalemate.

Our coaching was an opportunity to help her realize that her expectations from the past were actually causing her to get more pushback from others in the present than she would have otherwise. As we saw in Chapter 1, "Open," what is needed in conversations, especially those with people entrenched in their point of view, is to enter with a beginner's mind. I invited her to present a "clean slate" in every conversation. Realizing that she was carrying over her frustrations from past conversations into each new one, a lightbulb went on in her mind.

I then invited Marianne to put a boundary (in this case, a time limit) around individual conversations. I explained that when she provides a safe environment by listening, people won't ramble because they will feel they can express themselves fully and be heard. I then suggested she consider a different way of entering the conversations. I asked her to imagine what it would feel like to be "all ears" so that her curiosity and accepting presence could be palpably felt.

And I let her know that when she explored this new way of being, she could observe what was different for her and for her employees. Only from this space could a safe and effective solution be co-created for her team.

Not only did this method of being turn out to be more efficient, but it was also more effective and satisfying and created trust and loyalty that increased over time.

One of the hallmarks of yoga is that by engaging in postures, or *asanas,* we often feel physical discomfort. In yoga, we aim to go to the edge of this discomfort and pull back from it slightly so we can move the edge further out as we stretch and improve our muscle tone. These sensations are, by themselves, unremarkable. But for beginners, they often trigger thoughts that can be uncomfortable. This is caused by our overidentification with our bodies and the stories we have made up about them.

Marianne's team members were very much caught up in their fearful stories, and Marianne herself was caught up in her story of frustration with hearing their stories.

The next stage of yoga once you find the edge is to breathe directly into the discomfort. When we do this, we can simply observe it for what it is— pure physical sensation, without our own interpretation or story. We learn on the mat to "see what is as it is." We learn that we are not the bodies or the stories. Rather, we are the entity that witnesses the body and the story. By changing our identification, we stop judging ourselves and can neutrally observe and accept what is occurring. It is in this state of being that we are fully present. This is often referred to as "being the observer" or "being the witness."

The clean slate approach that Marianne took to conversations enabled her to be a witness to the concerns of her team as they were being expressed—not those of the day before or the week before that, and not some other team member's concerns but the individual's.

When we see the present moment through the filter of our past fears and future anxieties, we are solving problems using conditioned responses from a time that is "not now." Conversely, once we have a clear mind, we can move from a state that is filtered through our unconscious programming to a state that allows for a more objective assessment.

When we are in the moment and unbiased by our preprogrammed conditioning, we can see what is as it is. It is from this state of *witness consciousness,* unprejudiced by past experiences, that we can truly be present to solve problems. We transition from being a *reactive* perceiver to being a *witnessing* perceiver.

Witness consciousness is a prerequisite for effective leadership. When we possess it, we are unfettered and free to respond as necessary, allowing us not only to work with our minds, but also to access the innate intelligence within our bodies. This includes the ability to create, visualize, and synthesize. From the perspective of witness consciousness, we can access our body, mind, and heart and experience our universal energy flowing inside us. When we are in this state, we have the capacity to freely choose our actions. We can be responsive instead of reactive. We can access masterful leadership agility.

Don't mistake numbness for neutrality. Many leaders think of themselves as chess masters. They pride themselves on having risen to a high level of success by walling off all their human emotions, in essence compartmentalizing their pain so they can manage extraordinary feats of juggling and endurance. However, this suppressed numbness is not the same as being the witness. Many walled-off individuals may feel as if they are watching their lives fly by, not living them in their bodies.

The walled-off, cognitive view of leadership is a lonely one. Although we may initially feel safe and secure, we have created a moat around our castles and raised up the drawbridge to our lives. In this scenario, we have walled off our fears and anxieties while we live in a cognitive state. The "thinking and doing" have become the self-soothing balm that protects us from experiencing that which we have walled off. We soothe ourselves with our work so we won't be forced to experience who we are. *We are living as who we are not.* Decisions made from this perspective may be successful—in fact, many leaders are so sublimated that they have created a superpower.

However, the amount of emotional energy required to live in this space is exhausting. We are always on the alert for external "triggers" —the button-pushers who can draw us into the negative patterns of the past. Rather than digesting suffering once so we can let it pass, it can hurt us for the rest of our lives whenever we are triggered—and decisions made while suffering create ambiguous outcomes at best. In the process, our undigested trauma can traumatize others and destroy more relationships.

In the long run, it's not sustainable to live this way. At some point, leadership and life inevitably break down.

This protective armor, once created, is maintained until something breaks down in our lives. It may be our work, relationships, or health issues that serve as a catalyst. Something will force us to take a hard look at the price we are paying for that drawbridge being forever closed: the inability to truly experience our own best selves or to connect with others.

Even when successful, people who try to lead from this perspective create conflict with others. Leading requires connection, not isolation. Decisions made when leaders are isolated within their programmed, reactive minds never reflect their best. They are usually made while they are reactive and judgmental and often show that they do not trust others. Relationships with subordinates may be marked by conflict and lack creative problem solving. Leaders will be unable to adapt to a rapidly changing environment and will suffer, while blaming those around them for these failures. Such leaders are likely to be attached to the outcomes they create as a reflection of their self-worth. As no outcomes are ever perfect, they can never experience true satisfaction with themselves or others.

A leader who initiates action from a state of preconditioned programming creates confusion all around them. If they are divided from their inner source, they are not present at the moment. Their solutions will actually represent a solution to a problem from the past, not the one at hand. They will use an inner logic accessible only to the leader and visible only through the filters of the past. This type of leader seeks to solve their inner problems without doing their own work, usually with mediocre results.

Conversely, when a leader chooses to transition to witness consciousness, they can appreciate that *they* were the source of their own problem— and their own solutions. They realize that solving conflict starts first by solving it within yourself, and they no longer look to others to fix their problems. A leader who is aware of their own presence is connected to the power that lies within them.

Decisions made from witness consciousness will be harmonious. In this state, we draw on the brain as the equal of the heart, soul, and spirit, and we experience our entire being as a harmonious instrument. We are finally able to respond in the moment, unbiased by preconditioning. We accept others and inspire trust, and our relationships become peaceful. We inspire others to co-create with us. This generativity allows for rapid adaptation to change and innovation. We find joy in our choices, and our joy will be maintained regardless of outcomes.

If, at this point, you feel this being-based approach sounds too lofty, be patient with yourself. Trust the process. We will dive more deeply into the tools to help you "get there" in subsequent chapters. Hopefully by now you are curious enough to want to explore a new way of leading so that you can enjoy all the fruits your life has to offer.

The Effective Leader Works Within Their Circle of Influence

Is your focus on getting others to change more than on changing your own perspective? How many times have you tried to solve a problem by emphasizing what other people should do? We all do it. We do it with our co-workers, our partners, and our children. It feels easier (at least initially) than changing our personal role in the way things are. And it is completely futile.

We cannot force others to change. We cannot get from others what we have not first experienced within ourselves. We cannot create a relationship without conflict if we start in conflict within ourselves. We cannot co-create if we are not present for the "co" part of the act. From a place of our own direct experience, we can, however, *invite* others to change.

We do this by *being* an invitation. By opening our mind to the perspective of others, acknowledging their fears and worries, and listening to their dreams. When people feel heard, they don't expect us to agree with them. They just expect us to listen—without attachment to being right or changing them.

Easier said than done, right?

The reason this set of skills can feel difficult is that we've become accustomed to seeing our thought patterns as *who we are*. Over time, we've become identified with our habits of thought and attached to our ways of seeing. We want to be "right" or "in control" or "look good." Our identification with these patterns or structures forces us into repetitive loops in our communication and often damages our relationships.

Fortunately, this is not permanent! The potential to change these patterns is always available to us. All we have to do is initiate the inner call to evolve.

In business culture, it's common to talk about the scale or scope of a leader's influence. But the real circle of influence is much narrower than you may realize. *Your real circle of influence is just you. You are the only person you can influence as deeply as you need to. All other relationships you have are built outward from the inner circle of your being.*

If your internal mind-body-spirit system is imbalanced and misaligned, your presence in the world won't be very influential. You won't be able to hold the center, like the sun in the solar system that is your world. People won't know what you stand for, and they won't be able to locate you or be drawn to you as strongly.

However, once you are balanced and aligned internally, the energy of the people in your organization can align with yours, and you will begin to have greater reach through them.

Good knowledge and practices peel away false identities so our being can shine brightly and light up the world.

A Leader Must Take Radical Responsibility for Their Emotions and Thought Patterns

Are we practicing healthy, wise choices in food, rest, and exercise? The state of our physical body impacts our mental state and vice versa. Everything is connected. A conflict with others introduces conflict into your body, and conflict within the body can lead to conflict with others. When we feel poorly, it can cause us to damage our relationships with other people. Therefore, part of correct knowledge is understanding the importance of proper nutrition, rest, sleep, and correct breathing to develop and maintain our best leadership capacity. We must learn how to take good care of our physical bodies.

Writer Will Durant once summed up one of Aristotle's arguments as "We are what we repeatedly do.[5]" How do we begin to make these significant changes? We need to pay close attention to what we practice. Durant suggests "Excellence, then, is not an act, but a habit." Real change begins when we focus on creating awareness of our inside state. Begin by noticing. Ask yourself:

- "Where are my thoughts?"
- "Am I in *this* moment, or is my brain running into the future?"
- "What is within my own control right now?"

If you don't feel good, what is one thing you could do right now to feel a bit better—a bit more present in this moment—just one small thing? Do that for now. And then the next, and the next, and the next . . .

When we stop trying to be relatively better (better by comparison to another occasion) and become absolutely better (permanently and perpetually), we are living as an integrated person, with a connection to our presence, which is the source of self-acceptance and love. We will recognize the "being" quality within others and treat them as the human being they are rather than as an object. Those around us will feel what we are transmitting, and they will feel safe. This will activate the part of them that is present as well. From this state, all can create together with confidence, creativity, expediency, joy, adaptability, and, ultimately, success.

In summary, once we incorporate all these hallmarks into our communication, we will have learned how to be present—the precursor of all effective leadership. When we are in the present, unfettered by past experiences and unbiased by subconscious programming, only then can we see things as they are. It is only when we shift from "thinking and doing" (the sympathetic mode) to "feeling and being" (the parasympathetic mode) that we can use this relaxed, accepting presence to collaborate with others in a safe, effective, and joyous manner. It is when we shift from duality (living in sympathetic overdrive) to polarity (living in balance; neither for nor against what is happening now) that we can see, feel, and participate in the present with great clarity. This is the foundation of our birthright. It is a return home.

CHAPTER 3

Let Go
Explore Your Edges

If assumptions are questioned deeply enough, they let go of themselves.
The world becomes intelligible, kind, and problem-free,
because the mind has become clear.[1]

—STEPHEN MITCHELL

From a Western perspective, "letting go" is associated with unwinding from the stress and strain of our business lives, which we periodically do by going on vacation, getting a massage, or working out at the gym. Those methods are generally healthy. But their beneficial effect is temporary if we continue doing business in the

47

same manner. Let's be honest: How often do we return from a holiday only to feel even more stress and strain within 24 hours because we pick up right where we left off?

Letting go may also involve drinking alcohol, taking drugs, overeating, or indulging in a variety of other potentially addictive behaviors that we find self-soothing. The temporary relief we get from these unhealthy "solutions" is eclipsed by the fact that they compound our problems rather than solving them.

What happens when the effects of the alcohol wear off? We are wherever we were before our "escape," only now we also have a hangover. What happens after excessive consumption of sweet, salty, and fatty foods? We must contend with elevated cholesterol, inflammation, heart disease, obesity, and related conditions.

A real problem with reducing our stress through mood-altering substances and external soothing like shopping, gambling, and playing games on our smartphones is the potential for addiction. Even work can become an addiction when we use it to avoid facing our inner selves. Overwork seems to protect some people from the pain they wish to avoid. They labor for success to get a surge of biochemicals, like adrenaline or dopamine, in their bloodstream from rising to the challenge or "winning," not unlike test monkeys in a laboratory hitting a button over and over to get a banana.

A reason it's common to feel let down after we reach a goal or complete a project that we have worked hard or long on is that as our biochemistry rebalances, life seems less shiny. All the striving and pressure keep our focus on being happy in the future, not on the immediate pain we feel from the overwork—and not on a much healthier and more balanced experience of being joyful in each moment along the way. (Let's also not forget the toll overwork can take on our intimate relationships!)

None of the avoidance strategies or distractions we indulge in provides us with more than a temporary respite from the pain of any physical or psychic struggles that take place within us. At best, we may feel relatively better for a period. Then, after months and sometimes years, the pain eventually finds a way to get our attention—usually not in a way we welcome.

My clients, who are business leaders, frequently seek coaching when they are breaking down, whether the cause is physical, emotional, or relational. They reach out to me when, for them, the status quo is no longer tenable. They may have tried other solutions, but nothing has worked or they've reached the end of their rope.

Over the years, I have learned that the initial complaint a new client presents to me is rarely the real cause of their distress. They will tell me, "I'm here because my workers are disengaged," "My workload has become unmanageable and I need to learn to delegate better," "I have to develop a plan to attract new customers," or something else.

No matter what they say, the actual cause of their pain is not something or someone external that needs to be managed. Rather, it stems from their relationship to the problem—their internal reactions to those events and people. My role, as always, is to help them shift their gaze inward and begin to regulate their thoughts and energy.

Yoga offers an effective pathway to letting go of holding on to unwanted thoughts and emotions. From a yogic perspective, when we let go, we are freeing ourselves from getting stuck in the reactive, habitual tendencies that keep us trapped in repetitive thought and behavioral patterns. We may believe we are having an original experience and responding freshly, but if we haven't let go of our conditioned thoughts, we are fooling ourselves.

Letting go requires us to release the binds that keep us tied to memories and reactive patterns born from experiencing situations similar to our present ones. These patterns still live in our physical, mental, and energy bodies, so to make truly sustainable change, we need to let go on all those levels and become wiser about how we tend to be triggered.

Just as we can learn to identify when we are mentally and emotionally shut down and need to open, we can learn to recognize when the noise in our heads is too loud and chaotic or too circular, and we need to stop and let go. This can be done on the spot or as a routine step in a longer self-management process that's done daily or weekly, whichever is warranted by our state of being or can be accommodated in our schedule.

The process begins by peeling off one layer at a time, usually finding that there are many more layers underneath the surface when we let go of what we are conscious of. For this reason, letting go is a process that takes time, patience, courage, and self-compassion.

This may seem daunting. People are usually brought to this point because of pain or suffering and neither is pleasant to confront. But the rewards are worth it! At some stage, staying the same becomes more difficult than the prospect of change. The fear of injury from letting go is perceived as less than the pain of holding on. And there is even a kind of pleasure to be had from confronting things you would normally avoid.

Still, letting go doesn't have to be a painful or troubling experience. You might simply be curious about your patterns and enjoy the process of learning and growing. In that case, you may find it an illuminating technique that expands your self-knowledge.

No matter what, simply begin where you are right now—that's your perfect starting place. Let go of thoughts, feelings, and opinions about everything in front of you as part of an ongoing tidying up of your inner space so you can freshly experience each new moment.

LEADERSHIP IN ACTION

How Letting Go Helped Trisha Be at Peace in the Midst of Chaos

Trisha is a high-achieving professional woman in the legal arena. When she came to me for coaching, she described her day-to-day life as a "never-ending to-do list that depletes me." She was pondering a change, including a career transition, but felt "heavy and chained." She was afraid of needing to prove herself again and what would be involved in making her way in a new workplace. She was concerned about judgments she might face because of her choice to leave a lucrative job if she decided that was what she needed to do for herself. Added to this, Trisha was struggling to help some of her family members manage their behavioral health challenges.

Through our work together, Trisha learned the importance of self-care, including yoga, walks in parks, drawing, and more. She developed practices that helped her face her challenges at work and carried over into her homelife.

As a woman who relied on her strong intellect to do her work, learning the importance of managing and accessing her energy was critical for her. Bit by bit, she also learned the significance of feeling more relaxed and developed the ability to visualize and access positive images that stimulated her creativity. She described learning to accept herself and observe and then let go of the expectations she was "hooked into."

Letting go was the catalyst for eventual action. As Trisha learned to concentrate on releasing her expectations, she described feeling freer and having peace when surrounded by people with huge storms raging in their lives. She reported, "I am practicing quitting reacting in difficult situations and getting better at that. I can sit with the discomfort and let the toxicity pass through me. When the difficult encounter is over, as I go through my day, I have no more physical reactions. I am constantly aware of an impact I have had on someone else that didn't land where I wanted it to land. I now focus on what I can control, and I've learned that I can't control how things land. The key thing is to let other people's stuff flow through me. I've experienced it now. I know how to do it. Of everything, that's the nugget of pure gold."

Over the course of nine months, Trisha developed a vision to transition to an entirely new career that involves professional services outside the legal arena. In concluding our work, she said: "Your premise is you lead through inner peace. That's what I want to focus on now."

The Body Is the Gateway to Transitioning from Reactive to Responsive

In previous chapters, we've noted that the observer is intrinsic to our nature. We may believe that we are a particular way, yet if we draw back into the witnessing role, we can see that much of this identity is a cover for our true self, like a blanket, and blocks our perception of it.

Our covering personality is composed of our memories of past events, our reactions to those memories, stories we tell ourselves about our memories, and reactions to those stories. Different layers of cover come from our education, upbringing, culture, and societal and religious norms. These ingrained narratives, beliefs, and habitual reactions can stop us from seeing what is right in front of us as it is. Anything blocking the true self distorts reality.

The past replays itself. Fears born out of traumas small and large create anxiety in us about the future; if never properly "digested"—meaning mentally and emotionally processed and integrated or let go in their entirety—these traumas will replay themselves in our bodies again and again. Undigested fear or anxiety has a chemistry, a thought profile, an emotional profile, and therefore an embodied profile.

Energetically, a covering layer can come from our genetic profile and changes the expression of DNA at the epigenetic level, based on what our ancestors experienced. In other words, some of it comes from people we have never even met, extending back generations!

But no matter how, where, and when individual patterns entered us, all distort our ability to be present. Each of us interprets events through filters of which we are usually unaware.

The effects of patterns accumulate and get stored in our bodies, which are the densest level of our being. There is an inextricable link between our covering layers and physical discomfort. Everything we experience psychologically, chemically, and energetically is stored in our skeleton, fascia, muscles, organs, and nervous system, as well as in every cell in our bodies. Therefore, physical constriction and pain present us with opportunities to explore our underlying beliefs, thoughts, and narratives about our past experiences and our present-day stories.

The body is the true north of how much we have held onto or let go. It is neither for nor against anything. It simply reflects what is stored within us. As psychiatrist and renowned traumatic stress researcher Dr. Bessel van der Kolk writes, "The body keeps the score."[2]

To change our experience as leaders and people, we have to be willing to let go of it all—especially the fear of who we would be without our stories. This is why physically stretching our bodies, as we do on a yoga mat, is about more than becoming limber; it is also about moving the connective tissue and organs that feel stiff and stuck so we can release the old patterns of thought and emotion that are holding them in place.

When we stretch, we can attune ourselves to releasing trapped energy as well as tight, sore muscles and stiffness. As this energy is expelled, we can eliminate the patterns of thought and emotion at its core.

In yoga, it is understood that there are multiple layers of our being, which are increasingly subtle. (We'll talk about these in Chapter 4.) "According to the yoga tradition, every one of us has five bodies, each made of increasingly finer grades of energy," says Linda Johnsen in *Yoga International*. "These five bodies are called *koshas*, or 'sheaths,' in Sanskrit, because each fits in the next like a sword in a scabbard. Only the densest is made of matter as we know it; the other four are energy states invisible to the physical eye, though we can easily sense their presence inside us when we pay close attention. Since the inner bodies are the source of our well-being during life and are the vehicles in which we travel after death, India's ancient yogis developed specific exercises to strengthen and tone each one in turn."[3]

Each *kosha* has a similar manifestation of cover, as well as ways to release it. One prominent manifestation is a repetitive habit. As we have discussed previously, our habits help us minimize the energy expended by the brain when we're doing a productive, repetitive task, such as driving or brushing our teeth. We achieve the task competently through habits and can rely on them instinctually in an emergency.

However, some habits that conserve energy become negative. These habits help us avoid reexperiencing the trauma that was occurring when the covering belief or thought pattern was encoded by establishing fears, worries, and self-protective behaviors. In helping us avoid re-creating past suffering, these habits keep us from experiencing the present, which limits both our perception and our responses to people and conditions.

In other words, we end up exchanging one form of suffering for another! And we will continue suffering the effects of a covering pattern forever unless we learn how to let it go.

Think about your workplace. Was there ever a situation that wasn't working well, such as an employee who didn't suit your team's culture or a partnership that wasn't evolving the way you had hoped it would? Did you try to make it work beyond the point of comfort or reason? It is common to consume ourselves with trying to fix things and rearrange reality to avoid facing inner pain. What we don't realize is that in trying to protect ourselves from pain, not only do we perpetuate the pain, but we also build an extra layer of defenses and create adaptive strategies to contain it. The unintended consequence is that we amplify our suffering—and extend it to others.

If one person's past is arguing with another's and neither one is present to the now, it creates ineffective communication and conflict in the relationship. But when it is experienced in the present, discomfort is fleeting. If we can let go of our reaction to it and our resistance to feeling it, it only hurts for a moment. The physical discipline of yoga teaches us to observe and experience the discomfort of a posture as we are being challenged and then let it go. In this way, we do not suffer beyond the moment, and we do not introduce a new layer of covering belief.

As Temple of the Universe founder, author, and longtime yoga practitioner Michael A. Singer states eloquently in *The Untethered Soul,* "Everything will be okay as soon as you are okay with everything. And that's the only time everything will be okay."[4]

What Is "Letting Go"?

For our purposes, the term *letting go* refers to any process that removes a block or coverage that has prevented us from accessing our true nature. Blocks rob us of the ability to experience our presence because we are viewing life through the distorted lenses of the past and future. Blocks are stealthy, like thieves; they work undercover and overtime to steal our most precious asset: the present moment.

We are more than our memories and stored physical reactions to our experiences and memories. We have an innate capacity to feel, experience, and act spontaneously in the present moment. When the present is constricted by a continual replay of the past, we become trapped in the thickness of this blanket. *By letting go of who we are not, we reveal the true self.*

It is important to note that removing the coverage is not about letting go of the memories. We are simply releasing our *attachment* to those memories and to the stories about the memories that bind us to the past. Once a covering belief, thought, or feeling is released, we can be present psychologically and energetically.

Ideally, we would let go of being stuck and remove blocks in every layer of our being, from the densest to the subtlest. Letting go physically, as we aim to do on the yoga mat, is the first step and, for most of us, the easiest gateway to revealing the true self.

Even if you never choose to practice yoga, understanding basic yogic philosophy could help you learn to let go. And even if you've done yoga for years, open your mind to the possibility of learning something new here about how yoga can apply to your business activities.

The practice of physical yoga postures provides us with an accessible, tangible way to experience letting go. Having said this, many people find that the hardest step to take in yoga is the first one: getting onto the mat. There are many reasons we sometimes don't want to do it. The mind will make up all sorts of excuses. But they're just that—excuses.

Once you commit to honoring yourself by stepping onto the yoga mat, you can use the physical postures of yoga as they were designed: to become your own observer while you are preparing the body for meditation. One of the purposes of the postures is to provide us with an intense experience of sensations in the body, sometimes referred to as *going to the edge.*

Exploring Your Edge in Yoga as Training for Business and Life

The *edge* is the discomfort that a yoga practitioner explores when entering or withdrawing from their limits in a posture. This discomfort could be physical, mental, or emotional and is most likely a combination of the three. For example, if it is difficult to enter a posture on a certain day because our body is not as flexible as it was in the past, we may feel disappointed or frustrated. Or if we have discomfort that day, we may become worried about injuring ourselves. Mentally, we may compare ourselves negatively to others. We also might try to force our body to do something that doesn't come easily, only to be met with resistance and even pain. Then we will worry about the consequences.

When we feel uncomfortable, the mind can become distracted from the present experience. All kinds of ideas and images might get stirred up. It is easy to become absorbed in the antics of the "monkey mind," which routinely generates an average of 2,500 thoughts per hour! At the edge of our comfort zone on the yoga mat, it is natural to react to the intense sensations we feel with lots of mental chatter, including self-criticism. This is not yoga or *union with the true self*. This is separation and resistance to the moment.

Fortunately, such reactions are a gift! They offer us the first glimpse of awareness from which we can change our patterns of thought and perception and begin the process of letting go. Our first reaction isn't necessarily the best one, but it is our first opportunity to release a covering layer. We can only choose better if we know better.

The key to exploring the edge for the purpose of letting go is to see our first reaction with compassion for what it is: a reaction based on past, programmed conditioning, not an aware, conscious response to stress in the present moment.

In yoga, once we've accepted a reaction as such, we then refocus our attention on the sensations of discomfort, which *are* rooted in the present. Noticing these sensations brings us to the edge. The physical edge of discomfort attunes us to our *psychological edge* of discomfort as well. Realizing this, we can become curious about the edge. Can we feel it instead of labeling or judging it?

After going to the edge of our discomfort, we can purposefully back away from it slightly and explore it while we breathe into the stretch, a technique that creates a sense of safety in our nervous system. The mind becomes absorbed in the relaxed experience of sensation as we stay near the edge without forcing. At this point, mental chatter stops on its own, and the habitual anxious thoughts become less prominent. We are now present to what is in *this* moment.

In the process of relaxing and softening against the edge, we can observe our egoic, defensive self. We are no longer absorbed by the discomfort but instead have become its witness. We can choose to respond to the discomfort as an observer. We can use our breath and the depth of our physical posture to change the intensity of the discomfort.

When we relax our relationship to the edge of our discomfort, our experience of all sensations softens. As we relax, we enter into present-moment awareness. From our witness perspective, even when a habitual thought enters our mind, it no longer has the power to claim us. It is as if it is a passing cloud in the sky. This is how yoga is traditionally used to prepare a person for a practice in which they are relaxed and the observer "pump" is well-primed.

The point is that yoga on the mat helps us become the witness of the entire experience, including the sensations, the triggering stimuli, the thoughts, *and* the reactions.

It is only from this perspective of being a witness that we can respond rather than react. From the perspective of centered presence, we are in charge of our experience. We can choose to back out of a posture slightly or even completely, or we can choose to breathe into the discomfort and allow the body to find a new degree of flexibility and lightness in the pose.

From the witness perspective, we are able to:

- Notice that we are having a reaction to something
- Show compassion to ourselves for the human reactions we are having
- Observe with neutrality what is actually happening
- Choose an appropriate response for the moment

In this way, we experience the yogic pathway of shifting from an unconscious, habitual, preprogrammed reaction to the conscious ability to respond in the moment.

Yoga is wonderful training for handling the stressful elements of business and life with equanimity and poise. At the end of doing each pose on the mat, there is a moment of relaxation from the postural tension. This provides us with a brief opportunity to rest, but more important, what started as a painful energy blockage that may have been a source of discomfort in the posture is now transformed into a flow of released energy throughout the body. *Yoga transforms physical blocks into energetic releases and helps us convert stress that has been stored in our physical bodies from an undigested sympathetic nervous system response to a parasympathetic release of stress. In yoga, we release the sympathetically mediated stored fears and anxieties that keep us in the past or future, and activate the PSNS that keeps us relaxed and in the moment. As we eliminate the sympathetic holdings and tension in our bodies, the energy that is released can power our internal transformation. We can transmute the stored stress to a source of presence.*

As the observer, we are now present to the sensations of energy that constantly run throughout the body. We *become* the energy, no longer perceiving our self as separate from it. We turn inward and experience our energy bodies directly, so when we let go, we prepare ourselves to gain mastery over external influences. In Sanskrit, this turning inward is referred to as *pratyahara* ("withdrawal of the senses"). It is the fifth of the eight limbs of yoga codified by Patanjali in the *Yoga Sutras*.[5]

As our attention goes inward, we become absorbed in the experience of sensation in our bodies. We can easily dial into what we are feeling when our bodies are tense or relaxed, for example. It is precisely when this attunement to internal sensation begins—and we become fully occupied by these sensations—that we stop attending to our thoughts and are no longer gripped by conditioned responses. We are fully in the present moment once we let go.

Life Is Your Yoga Mat

If you have no desire to add a yoga mat to your lifestyle, have no worries. Life provides all sorts of uncomfortable "edges" on which to practice becoming an observer! Edges aren't necessarily limited to noticing your discomfort with bodily sensations. They can come from external sources as well. An edge can be anything from a colleague who never follows through on their promises to a demanding customer, a cash-flow crunch, a long line in a store, a recorded phone menu with eight dead-end options, conflicting commitments between your work and your personal life, or challenging relationships. The list of possible edges is endless. Once you learn to recognize an edge, you will see them everywhere.

Although having a physical yoga practice makes it easier to become aware of your edges, it is not required for learning to let go. Edges extend far beyond the yoga mat.

Now here's the tricky part. Just as getting on the yoga mat may repel you because it triggers negative internal reactions, it can also be difficult to approach the challenges of the world as yet another version of the yoga mat. Maintaining a constant state of awareness can be fatiguing, especially when you're just learning how.

But what if, instead of reacting to endless frustrating moments throughout your day, you could instead treat those moments *as if* you were on a yoga mat? And when you made this mental shift, you could breathe into, and back away from, the discomfort of any moment?

We *can* do this, freely and by choice. We can go from a reactive state to becoming the observer or witness of any moment. We can even use the opportunity to thank those who push our buttons for revealing what our buttons are and teaching us to become observers of ourselves in a state of reaction.

Once we become the observer, we can choose a healthy response for the moment rather than reacting in a hasty, thoughtless manner that could result in misunderstandings, hurt feelings, mistakes and accidents, regrets, and other unwanted or negative consequences. When a stressful situation is behind us, if we chose to respond rather than react, we can look back and feel that we have released discomfort on one or even multiple levels: physical, mental, emotional, or a combination of some or all of those. What started as a frustrating experience in button pushing thus became an opportunity to practice our own transformation.

The best things about exploring the edges in life? It's always available to us, it doesn't cost anything, we can take it anywhere, and it can never be lost or taken away.

Over time, we will learn that the root of all the reactions we thought were coming from outside us is actually created within us.

The ability to transform our own resistance and tension into neutrality is critical for leadership. Letting go is therefore an important skill. For one, it allows a leader to negate the reactive or triggered responses that occur when their fears are placed on another person. We want our leaders to accept people as they are instead of allowing their fears and anxieties to influence their view of others. A leader who is present and neutral can do this. For another, leaders who are "in neutral"—like a car that is prepared to quickly shift into gear—can move in any direction that is required. After letting go, leaders are nimble in thought and in action. In other words, leaders who bring themselves into the present moment and let go of the preconditioned mental habits from the past can choose their gear and direction to match the energy of the moment.

In addition, letting go helps leaders reduce the impact of stress on their bodies. Healthy tension is part of polarity—the dynamic ability to go to extremes on either side of the sympathetic-parasympathetic spectrum and return quickly to balance afterward. We can use polarity to create. As we discussed in Chapter 2, stress has biological and psychological components that create emotional indigestion. This results from years of poor food habits, emotional dysregulation, and unhealthy patterns of thought. In time, this buildup becomes so great that it cannot be eliminated by the body, and we lose equilibrium as these unmitigated imbalances create stored tension. We experience this tension as pain, conflict, and suffering.

This stress is initiated within us. When we lead from the inner space of conflict, we provoke conflict from others instead of inspiring collaboration.

Healthy tension helps us express the things that matter to us, but this kind of pressure is temporary, not chronic. Unhealthy, long-term tension creates stress and often constriction. Leaders who let go create space for the people they work, enhancing the creativity of others. Letting go helps leaders deal creatively with change and disruption when they are seeking new ways of solving an old problem.

LEADERSHIP IN ACTION
A Leadership Case Study of Letting Go

Keith was the founder of a successful, growing entrepreneurial venture. He came to me for coaching because he was experiencing numerous conflicts in the workplace and at home. His colleagues and direct reports were frustrated, and his marriage was strained.

Keith had a typical business founder's profile: He had the vision to build an organization from scratch that would meet a need. The company was now at the stage where, for it to grow, he needed to learn how to delegate to other members of his team. But he was having trouble relinquishing control. Letting go of certain tasks was becoming an internal as much as an external requirement—he needed to let go of having everything done *his way* by others. His staff reported to me that Keith was often critical of them. He said he was frustrated at their failure to step up enough.

At the time we began our work together, Keith was using a highly directive leadership style, one I often observe in leaders who have not yet had leadership coaching. He also had grown up in a command-and-control household, in which family members had to do things in the expected way. Now, many years later, Keith's subconscious mind had translated his familial memories into a habit of expressing intense judgments of people in his workplace. The belief structures from his formative years were blocking creative communication with those he depended on to move the company forward. Without that, the organization's ability to produce consistently great results had stalled.

When we began exploring the concept of letting go, Keith was extremely uncomfortable. Although open to change, his strong tendencies to control others with an authoritative, overbearing manner made him unable to invite others to hold open, productive conversations with him. His judgments of them and himself were standing in the way. He was as yet unaware of how the self-critical judgments he had formed in reaction to events in his past were creating dysfunction in his relationships.

Keith came to me with a strong desire to be, in his words, a "higher-level leader." We began by helping him learn to notice sensations in his body with curiosity. He then explored his inner landscape in a nonjudgmental, compassionate way, using his breath as a way to create expanded awareness of what he was feeling emotionally. This led to him developing an ability to calm himself and become less reactive in disappointing situations.

As a result, Keith noted, "I'm redefining myself. It's like me becoming me. I have compassion for myself. In these moments of calm and quiet, I'm aware of my mood and attitude. I set that tone, and then I have a curiosity toward others. I see that compassion starts with me."

He indicated that by gradually learning to slow down, be open, and control his reactions, he was more in the moment. "When I do these things," he said, "I show up as confident and comfortable. Through this process, my subconscious is revealing itself to me, and that is magical!"

Over a six-month period, Keith reported experiencing heightened awareness, improved moods, and increased energy. He wasn't taking things as personally as before. Practicing letting go, including developing compassion for himself, was allowing him to relax. In one of our phone sessions, he told me, "If I wake up feeling angry, I use the technique for letting go that you taught me, so I start my day with the right energy. This is so big for me. I see now that my work is in managing my own energy. By being present, I can be at peace without expectation.

"In the midst of difficult times, I repeat, 'And I breathe,' while focusing on letting go of the external worries. My strongest realization has been that I cannot escape reality, but I can escape being tortured by the past and fears of the future."

Keith went on to say, "I've learned that the power I bring to conversations goes far beyond the words I speak. One of the biggest blockages I see in communication between members of my team is how there is reactivity everywhere. For me, the reactivity comes from having answers (or wanting to skip ahead to answers) instead of posing questions."

Keith and I did some role-playing with archetypes that allowed him to recognize the difference between judging/reacting and curious/compassionate responding. Knowing what signals to watch for in various types of interactions enabled him to quickly let go of judgments on the spot and back off from his expectations when he could see they were causing him and others discomfort.

He summed up his new intentions this way: "We were never trained as listeners. We were celebrated as actors for our bravado. We're not reinforced for creating space, compassion, and energy. My personal goal is to turn compassion into an action verb."

By the way, this role-playing exercise is something that you, as a leader, can do with members of your team when you see signs of reactivity erupting in their exchanges. Be sure to establish a safe space for team collaboration, as that sets the foundation for harmony and co-creativity.

Keith went on to successfully lead his company through an acquisition. The company went to the next level of its potential, and he and other owners received significant returns on their early investments. He was so inspired by what he learned from navigating this liquidity event that he went on to start a new career as a consultant to help other entrepreneurs.

How frequently does a leader invite a consultant or coach into their organization and ask them to start working with their team? They often don't realize the connection between how *they* are being and how the team is relating to them. It feels like "I'm OK. You're not OK." Leaders with this blind spot believe that learning new ways is best done by the people in the trenches, but this approach defies the laws of leadership physics—that somehow there is an "us" or "me" and an "everyone else." This is simply not true.

Organizations are unified fields of energy. They are complex systems made up of networks of people in relationships. The connections are expressed through conversations, memos, and the sharing of energy. Leaders who are bound up in the past are burdening these connections with their habits. When a leader can shift away from their conditioned way of reacting to a conscious, in-the-now response, they will experience entirely different conversations. When leaders share energy and information that is grounded in the present, others will engage with them differently.

When we are consumed by frustration or anger, for example, our emotions become heightened, and our energy reflects this amplified emotional intensity. Our stressed internal landscape is easily perceived and felt by those around us. When this happens, the feedback we stimulate in others often mirrors our internal landscape.

Our energy and emotions are contagious!

Letting go is a physical, mental, emotional, and energetic process. We learn to let go by paying attention to our bodily sensations because pure sensations reflect our other holding patterns. The physical body reflects the mental body and the emotional body—and every other body or level of awareness in our experience, from the densest to the subtlest. When our physical form feels discomfort or pain, it may be a clue that we are resisting something. Therefore, when we let go of this coverage, this resistance, we may experience relief. If there was pain or discomfort previously, it often subsides, along with the emotional attachment that came from the mistaken perception that the source of the discomfort lay outside us.

There will likely be emotional relief as well. Usually physical bracing, especially tension in the back, reflects emotional holding on a subconscious level. Stiffening up is a recognized aspect of the fight-or-flight response. When we let go, we put our entire being into a sort of neutral zone. This relaxed, open state of being is necessary for effective leadership and collaboration with others.

Letting go allows us to avoid the impact of a karmic boomerang when what appears to be triggered by external forces is that which is actually within us all along. When a leader lets go, they can convert a conflict-creating relationship into one of conscious communication and co-creation.

When leaders are presented with a significant event or crisis, they may need to explore how to deal with change. This usually involves being open to entirely new ways of working. How can a leader set the stage for embracing new possibilities if they are hooked into their own entrenched habits of thought and emotion? The agility that is required simply won't be available. For an organization to learn how to do this, the leader will have to go first and show the rest how to embody the letting-go experience.

Can you think of a time or two when you had the experience I'm describing? If you have any regrets about such a period or wish you could have handled the change more expertly and gracefully, the technique I'm going to give you below will help you handle similar events in the future.

Letting go is a skill that can be learned, and it's too bad most of us aren't taught it at a parent's knee. Just as learning any skill, like playing a sport, requires repetition, so does training the mind and body to let go. We need to practice the skill frequently, and preferably "off the field," at a time when we are generally relaxed rather than "in the game" of life, where the stakes are high. While our emotions and nerves are in play, it can be much harder to do.

Once you can successfully let go, you're much more likely to be able to do it in real life, when you actually need to score a point.

Where should you practice? Well, the yoga mat is a terrific place for relaxed practice sessions, but if you're not so inclined, there is another way to learn letting go that I recommend, which is visualization.

Below you'll find one technique for visualization and one physical practice to help you learn to let go.

The Letting Go Visualization Workout

To visualize for the sake of strengthening your capacity to let go, consider a few of the most common scenarios that are emotionally challenging for you, such as meetings, phone calls, live presentations, and so on. The point is to get a clear picture in your mind of the difficult context in which you will be operating.

Step 1: Your Body. Explore the internal state and responses of your physical body as you imagine living through an experience that perturbs you. What sensations have your thoughts about this situation created within you? Do you feel discomfort or pain?

Observe what happens without label or judgment. Be curious as to the pure sensations you feel, evaluating them simply as what they are—signals from your body. Are the signals strong in a particular area, such as your neck, gut, heart, or lower back?

Breathe deeply into the space of the discomfort you perceive. Exhale slowly. Notice what happens at the edges of the discomfort as you do. Is it releasing a little bit?

Step 2: Your Mind. Continuing to visualize the same scenario, now check in with your mind. Where are your thoughts? What are you focusing on in this experience? What do you think you might be holding on to from a similar past experience? Are you distracted by the activity of your mind? Is your mental activity quiet or busy? Are your thoughts racing?

Breathe in deeply. Exhale slowly. Notice what happens in your headspace as you do. Is there an effect on your mind? Is the activity in your mind ceasing or slowing, even a little?

Step 3: Your Emotions. Finally, explore your emotions. Name the top one or two you observe without labeling or judging them. Just notice them from a posture of curiosity. Keep belly-breathing and do your best to stay relaxed as you do.

Step 4: Inquire. Once you've become present to all you are experiencing, you can do some radical self-inquiry. Ask: "What do I need right now in order to let go?"

An answer will come.

Your body may offer the first clue. Just listen to whatever form it comes to you in. It may offer you a sensation or a color, or you might hear a word or see a picture in your head. The body has its own special language for communication. Notice the calm you experience when you proceed by paying attention to the body. Notice the thoughts and emotions settle in.

Or you can begin with your emotions and allow the body to follow.

If you find yourself having negative expectations of another person, do your best to visualize them from a place of acceptance and neutrality. The brain often does not distinguish between the imagination and reality. Consider how your body responds to a nightmare when you wake up and your heart is racing, or when you see a horror movie and break into a cold sweat. Athletes often use visualization as an effective way to train their motor skills, and it can be a powerful way to retrain the brain and body. It can also be helpful for practicing letting go.

There is no right or wrong way to practice the art of letting go. I have found, however, that allowing the body to take the lead is usually the quickest and most dependable option, as *the body never lies.* It doesn't know how to mislead us. The mind, on the other hand, is a trickster. It expertly creates stories, illusions, and justifications to create a perception of "safety." But these become tired, worn, and unproductive over time. Viewing the body as true north on our compass is not only simple, but also 100 percent reliable.

The internal agitation a leader may experience can usually be mitigated through an effective check-in system such as this one. But it requires consistent practice to get good at it. Once you become skilled in letting go, you will be able to do it on the spot in an instant without anyone being the wiser. It can become a great buffer against inflamed, reactive impulses, which unchecked might cause us to say and do things in the heat of the moment that we later regret.

Beyond leading in a crisis, think of all the other ways this workout could be helpful to you. Letting go allows us to strip away the illusion that we are in control. It doesn't mean we let go of the expectation of performance from others, but it does mean we are not in control of what they do. Instead, we focus on letting go of our internal holding patterns—physical, mental, and emotional—that stop us from being present to others where they are right now. When we stop expecting them to behave in the way we think they ought to, we can start to truly connect with them as they are. Out of this connection, new possibilities for mutual agreements, innovation, and co-creation that were previously unimaginable will spring forth. By letting go of our self-imposed limitations, we allow others to have break-throughs and go further ourselves.

The Seated Forward Bend: A Physical Practice of Letting Go

Here is a simple yoga stretch you can do to experience your edge within your body and learn to let go. Physically, approach this stretch with gentleness and self-compassion. Mentally, aim to be with what is. The pose is intended to be restorative and relaxing once you have settled into it.

EXERCISE 4: **Physical Practice of Letting Go**

Modification: You may wish to use props to support your body weight when you are bent forward if your back is very tight and inflexible. In this case, try stacking a padded yoga bolster or a couple of soft pillows in your lap or on your legs to rest your chest and forehead on. Some people are almost sitting upright when they stretch forward at first. Whatever you need to do is OK.

1. Sit on the floor with your legs outstretched directly in front of you. Your knees should be facing upward rather than turning out to the sides. It can help to gently flex your feet, but do not lock your knees. This is a no-force, no-strain exercise.

2. Inhale deeply through your nose while feeling your abdomen expand. While you reach your arms up overhead, keep your shoulders relaxed and down.

3. As you exhale, gradually begin to reach forward from your hip creases and drape your body over your legs, carefully leading with your sternum and without rounding your back. Go until you feel the first edge—a place where you would need to exert yourself or push to go any further. Stay there and relax as best you can, breathing normally.

4. Notice any sensations you feel without labeling or judging them.

5. Become the witness of the psychological edge of your discomfort. What emotions are there?

EXERCISE 4: **Physical Practice of Letting Go, cont.**

6. Breathe more deeply now, inhaling through the nose, feeling the abdomen expand.

7. Exhale very slowly. Then hold the exhale as long as you can without effort.

8. Drop your sternum further forward until you feel the next edge.

9. Continue releasing in the same fashion until you have gotten your chest as close to your outstretched legs as you can without strain. At some point, your arms may come to rest on your legs or the floor beside your legs.

10. When you feel ready, sit up straight, placing your arms at your side. Slowly lie down on your back with your feet on the floor and knees pointed toward the ceiling. Simply feel the sensations.

Release your mind through letting go, and your body will follow. The body will sometimes allow what the mind will not, so as you practice releasing at the edge in this stretch, you will begin to understand how to be with different kinds of experiences, even those that feel difficult and frightening, without becoming reactive and resistant. Go slowly and keep breathing. You will notice that you are safe at the edge, and that will train your nervous system to remain open and calm under pressure.

The body has an innate protective mechanism, the *myotatic reflex,* that kicks in when muscles are being stretched to their limit.[6] The stretch prompts an automatic contraction of muscles to inhibit further movement and prevent injury. By breathing and relaxing at your edge, the contraction will end, and then the stretch can spontaneously deepen. Abrupt movement or force may reengage the contraction. The goal is to let go of attempting to control your body. As you relax into the posture, the stuck energy is released, and you will feel your body returning to its natural state of homeostatic balance.

Rising Up by Letting Go

Letting go is a hallmark of leaders who have created a positive relationship with themselves. When a leader lets go, they can extend that relationship to others. Within just two to three months of our working on this, Keith noticed that the agitation and stress he had been experiencing calmed down. He could see what is as it is. From this new vantage point, Keith could communicate more effectively with colleagues and team members about important goals and potential courses of action. This, in turn, helped others come onboard because everyone was speaking in "real present time" instead of in terms of the past or the future. Such benchmarks are the precursors to effective leadership and influence.

Even if we let go daily, we will still have goals, standards, and outcomes we desire. But we will have the ability to create new, more open conversations where we can listen deeply to others, offer them our presence, and collaborate effectively with them. Being a good leader isn't about being right or telling others what to do. It's about being present in the current conversation, at this moment, and seeing the humanity of the person or team in front of us.

Letting go means to go beyond, where there is no "good" or "bad," no "for" or "against," no "I'm right" or "you're wrong." There is just being present—in the present. When everyone can do this, we will lead in a way that reflects our shared humanity. This is my vision for leadership in the 21st century.

CHAPTER 4

Drop In
Shift from Doing to Nondoing

I look at these things with intense delight and
as I observe them there is no observer
but only sheer beauty like love.

—JIDDU KRISHNAMURTI

A leader's true power comes from something that often cannot be seen, although it certainly can always be felt: the gift of presence.

By contrast, we can both *see* and *feel* a lack of presence in another person. We observe the absence when the person with whom we are speaking is looking at something else or when their eyes flutter quickly. We also observe when someone is speaking so quickly that they're not creating enough space for us to respond. All these things, among others, demonstrate a lack of presence.

Lack of presence creates distance, distress, and disconnection in our relationships.

Presence is the opposite. We see it when there is strong eye contact with another person. We see it when they are relaxed and breathing in a natural rhythm as we speak. We feel it when there is space enough for us to offer our thoughts and feelings in between their comments without interruption.

Presence is the most valuable leadership gift we have to offer. It is precious and rare, but few people know they can tap into it, and even fewer know how to sustain it throughout a hectic workday.

Presence is easily accessed through the yogic technique of *dropping in*. From the yogic perspective, dropping in is the transformation from lack of presence to the state of being *centered and present*. When we drop in, we are centered because we are connected to our own energy. We find ourselves in a neutral mental space in which we are neither for nor against what is. A centered person can witness what is without the need to judge or force things. After we drop in, we can see what is in the moment, exactly as it is.

How We Are Absent in the Present at Work

Leaders often ask outside consultants to find ways to improve productivity or efficiency. Often these experts uncover real, systemic problems, reinforcing the leader's belief that the answers they need will come from outside. However, even after making the recommended fixes, many of them still experience ongoing failures in teamwork, communication, and productivity. Their organizations continue to suffer from high turnover due to worker dissatisfaction. Why?

In my experience as an executive coach, the answer lies within the leaders. They often tolerate deficits in themselves while blaming everything and everyone around them for their poor outcomes. In fact, people throughout an organization can get stuck in the victim perspective.

Such mental distortions can make it nearly impossible to create and maintain breakthrough results.

We often forget how much personal power we really have—we can wreak havoc within an organization when we can't deploy our own energy effectively. Leaders and teams that don't understand the importance of their personal presence cannot communicate well with one another. And when team members don't connect safely and openly, the result is a lack of trust and a failure to produce consistent results.

Because they set the tone for company culture, leaders have a responsibility to intentionally create an effective organizational ecosystem. Yet we often see them do the opposite. This isn't because they get out of bed in the morning and think, *How can I go to work today and create disengagement and chaos?* They are simply unaware that an unconscious mind, left to its programmed habits, creates internal chaos that then spreads throughout the organization at large.

When we see persistent chaos in a team, it is a sign that the leader is running on mental software from the past, conjuring up associated emotions and reactions that may have made sense at an earlier time, even if they are unsuitable for the moment at hand. By running old programs, leaders unwittingly create unconscious, unhappy, and untenable workplaces.

Developing leadership presence is critical to improving the state of today's organizations, which are characterized by reactivity, firefighting, and burnout. Distraction, disconnection, and disengagement have become the accepted norm. A 2022 Gallup study showed that only 32 percent of U.S. workers are engaged in their work![1]

Although some workplaces create environments that attempt to offer workers respite, including free massages, table tennis, and cafés, these perks are insufficient to help workers cope. These methods can certainly help people reconnect with their bodies and may even create a physical space where they can easily connect with others. Unfortunately, this type of support doesn't solve the underlying cause of disconnection: a lack of presence.

Without getting to the root of many of today's most pressing leadership problems, we can expect continued deterioration in worker engagement, satisfaction, and loyalty because it is happening at a time when the technology we use to conduct our business is placing a heavy burden on the human nervous system. The same technology that is speeding our business transactions and connecting people everywhere is contributing to our withdrawal from the natural world. Our bodies were not designed for the complexity of mental stimulation we face every day. Without the grounding presence of genuine human connection, regular contact with nature, and deeper communication, we accumulate more stress than our body wiring can accommodate. We're overwhelmed!

The typical day of a Western leader starts with waking up to an alarm, turning on our phone to check for urgent communications, possibly working out, eating breakfast while reading or watching the news (often fear-based stories filled with violent images), and saying goodbye to loved ones without being conscious of how they or we feel. We then may face a commute to work while drinking coffee and talking on a cell phone. We use the "dead time" of rush hour to solve business or personal problems, congratulating ourselves for our efficiency. By the time we arrive at the office, we feel totally prepared, charged up, and ready to go. We are so ready, in fact, that most of us have already left—our presence!

As soon as we awaken, we begin the process of separation from the unconscious mind we possess during sleep. The alarm clock's jolt triggers a fight-or-flight response, setting off a chain reaction that continues when we amplify the disconnection with everything else I've just described.

Imagine going through life with nearsightedness or farsightedness and not having access to eyeglasses or contact lenses. Everything would appear distorted. This is comparable to how most of us live!

In the West, we believe being *ready to go* means fully activating the sympathetic nervous system. Some days we can be activated continuously from the moment the alarm goes off in the morning until we go to sleep at night. But the sympathetic nervous system (SNS) really is designed to handle only short bursts of fight-or-flight chemistry. Under normal circumstances, the body relaxes 20 to 30 minutes after a threat has passed and returns to its normal state. Those of us who experience insomnia may owe it to a chronically supercharged sympathetic state that has not been balanced effectively—and to the caffeine we then consume to override our fatigue. All the alcohol, pills, and other substances in the world won't fix what ails us, as these are only crutches to artificially sustain an unstable and compromised lifestyle.

While prepping to greet our challenges, we leave out the most important step: connecting with *ourselves* so we can be present internally before leaving home to meet with others. And we sacrifice the best part of the day when we begin our morning this way.

When we arrive at work with our brain in a supercharged reactive state, we are not truly present. Habitual thoughts and actions based on our past fears and future anxieties will create the same thoughts and actions as the day before. This will continue into the next day and the day after that because we tend to reenact the actions of the past.

When our mental and emotional conditioning is reflected in our reactions, we can be sure we are responding to projections from memory. If we are reacting to a projection, we are not seeing reality. Conditioned eyes only see distortions. Based on distorted perceptions, we build new distorted realities on the older ones. It's impossible to break the cycle until we can see reality clearly, without filters.

But how?

Break Out of Your Distortions to Drop into Your Presence

Learning how to become present is one of the most critical competencies for 21st-century leaders. In a chaotic, rapidly changing world, your centered presence may be the single best gift you can give to yourself and others. Any problem you solve with a reactive mind can, at best, only make you feel and perform *relatively* better. But when you're present, you're *absolutely* better—functioning well regardless of outcomes or circumstances.

Fortunately, yogic wisdom offers us a valuable framework for understanding reality. Instead of immersing yourself in the world's distractions, this framework is an opportunity to withdraw your senses from the external world and look within yourself. Dropping into yourself— into your true being at the center of all you are—is a chance to shift your perspective. Once you have dropped in, you can easily move from seeing a problem and its solution as *outside* you to seeing that they lie *within* you.

This is important to leadership because the biggest leap we can make in engagement and productivity comes from shifting our internal awareness away from a reactive lens. Any time we try to solve a problem reactively, the solution has an external focus. But the root of the problem is never the outside world but the biased perceiver that lives within us all. Once we recognize this, we can learn to shift our perspective to become a perceiver without judgment or bias.

Cultivate Your Body's Wisdom

In the West, the prevailing view is that wisdom comes from the mind. Many of us were raised without any acknowledgment of the importance of paying attention to our bodies. We literally experience the world entirely in our heads, as if they are stuck on top of our bodies with no connection between the brain and our limbs and other body parts!

Nothing could be further from the truth. The West is increasingly receptive to revisiting ancient teachings about energy modalities, including yoga, tai chi, Jin Shin Jyutsu, Reiki, and other ancient systems from the East. Many people have found these beneficial for healing. These systems have most often been relegated to the domain of health and well-being and not integrated into business per se. It is only recently that there has been interest in their application to all aspects of Western life.

Leaders will benefit from learning to attune to their own presence while modeling it for others. To effectively influence others, they must first be present and become aware of their bodies and the energy they are emitting.

The body offers a living laboratory in which to investigate our mental and emotional states. By getting in touch with our primary bodily sensations, not our commentary on our sensations, we can explore our relationship to self and others as a gateway to presence. This is why having a somatic practice (sōma is Greek for "body") is essential. We can all feel, notice, and experience sensations in the body. When we do, we are accessing the body and its energy in pure form, without the shackles that come from thought.

Our brains spontaneously generate thousands of thoughts per day, most of which are random. We believe we are conscious and rational, yet the vast majority of our thoughts are habitual and repetitive—not conscious. Our neural pathways are like train tracks, and we can be runaway trains, careening down a track at high speed without working brakes!

We've had our entire lifetime to build the tracks and pathways for our thoughts. They have been laid down on top of our age, family history, education, gender, religious beliefs, and geographical location, among other things. Our tracks include our past fears and memories and our worries about the future. They reliably lead us to the same stations over and over.

How to Respond vs. React for Leadership Effectiveness

Emotions are among the most important human expressions. Because they consist of energy, emotions are constantly moving and changing. If we understand this, we have the ability to choose what we do with the spontaneous emotions that arise.

Thoughts and emotions are reciprocal. A thought can trigger emotion, and emotion can trigger thought. If we allow our thoughts to spiral, soon we are going deep down a rabbit hole of whatever problem or feeling has seized our attention. In the event of one of these *amygdala hijacks,* we have an overwhelming emotional response. Mentally, it is as if we have left our body for a few seconds. We are unable to respond rationally because we have vacated our ability to be present to what is happening. We are unconscious while awake.

When leaders get caught in emotional reactivity, they cannot be effective.

Consider Amanda, a CEO who was having difficulty in a relationship with a partner company. Everything was going really well in the relationships with all the divisions of the company—except for one. She had received word that this one division might be challenging for her because of an individual whose goals and desires were not aligned with hers. She was upset.

She told me, "I wake up and I'm stressed. My jaw is clenched, I have insomnia, and I don't know what to do." She was clearly in a high-alert, high-reactive mode—a runaway train.

I said, "From this place that you're in right now, you will have difficulty imagining the right solution. But if you can get into a relaxed state, a range of possibilities may emerge."

When I guided her through an exercise to help her drop in, she was able to access her body's innate intelligence immediately and effortlessly. As a result of being relaxed and expansive, she discovered a way to move forward that felt solid and effective. She was confident in the appropriateness of the solution that presented itself. She became clear that she needed to have a specific conversation she had not yet had. She also appreciated the way of being she needed to bring to the conversation. When she met with her colleague in this new manner, the other individual was more open than she had imagined. Things at work began to shift. Not surprisingly, her sleep quality improved as well.

The balance of sympathetic and parasympathetic states is critical both for our well-being and for the cultivation of presence. Neither state is superior to the other. They are opposite and equal in their importance. Both are needed to dynamically maintain the homeostasis of the body. (Remember, a state of polarity is the ability to go from one state to the other in alternation, as needed.) As with any ecosystem, complementary forces are necessary to preserve harmony.

The trouble is that our regular *thinking* and *doing* in the world of business are *sympathetically* activating. It is not possible to use *only* the mind to become relaxed and restore balance to the nervous system. We need to counterbalance our SNS activation through *feeling* and *being*. This is a whole new mode that many high-powered leaders are less familiar with and may not entirely trust.

The good news, however, is that when we are in a relaxed, parasympathetic state, we can access the capabilities of our higher intelligence that we need for presence and collaboration, such as visualization and spontaneous generative creativity. As we move from sympathetic to parasympathetic activation, we move from action (fight or flight) to metabolism (rest and digest), from tension to relaxation, from logic to intuition, from contraction/guardedness to expansion/openness, from forcing to allowing, from judgment to acceptance, from programmed thought patterns to present-moment thoughts infused with inspiration, from thinking and doing to feeling and being, from ego to witness.

What a Piece of Work Are We!

The brain is both our greatest gift and our greatest challenge. Gaining mastery over our mental distortions is a key skill in avoiding suffering and is the crux of effective leadership.

The brain can trick our bodies into remaining in a chronic sympathetic state, even if no life-threatening problems exist, as we've discussed. The predominant state of most modern humans is one of sympathetic overdrive, causing an imbalance of our natural homeostatic systems and leading to chronic stress-related conditions.[2]

Given that the nature of the human condition is the sympathetic state, most techniques for achieving internal balance are focused on elevating the parasympathetic nervous system (PSNS) and decreasing the activity of the sympathetic nervous system (SNS). Many practitioners of these techniques can get themselves into a deeply parasympathetic state. However, for a business leader who has to actively solve problems, this would not be particularly useful, as dealing with complex business issues in a deeply relaxed state might not turn out so well. For a high-performing individual, something else is required—an alert yet calm wakefulness.

How do you solve a problem from a state designed to help you *not* do things?

The goal is to pass through this state of "nondoing" and then maintain that calm mental posture while in action. As tranquility and healing occur when the body is in balance, we can achieve that point of tranquility by dropping in. When we do this, our SNS and PSNS are *equally* activated—a state we call *integrated homeostasis*.

Our bodies, when integrated and functioning well in polarity, are supercomputers that can receive, send, and process information in multiple dimensions at the same time. When we have dropped into polarity, we are receiving, processing, and disseminating information using our full human capacities, not just those of a brain that has distorted processing problems. When we work to create the balance we need within ourselves, we can engage with others with all our faculties in harmony.

After dropping in, we have access to intelligence that transcends the cognitive, thinking mind. When we drop in, we befriend our body and its innate wisdom. In time, we learn to trust that dropping in helps us access our powerful inner compass.

But before we can change our state, we need to become aware of the state we are currently in—so it is useful to inventory the different levels of our being.

The Anatomy of Our Energy System: The Five *Koshas* or Dimensions of Awareness

Yoga teaches that we experience the world through five layers of awareness, or *koshas, which means "sheaths."* The densest, most tangible layer is physical, while the other layers are not visible and are progressively more subtle. Sometimes these are described as *energy sheaths* or *sheaths of existence.*

We can only see the visible layer of our being, the physical body. The others are invisible to the naked eye, but we can sense them all once we learn how. A disturbance in any of the five layers of awareness affects all the others. As we become more proficient at sensing them, we will have opportunities to remove blockages to these layers through the same practices that help us become more self-aware, including breathing, holding certain postures, and meditation. When we do the practices successfully, we gain access to our true self, or soul (*atman* in Sanskrit).

In order from densest to subtlest, the five sheaths of awareness are:

1. The physical sheath, the *annamaya kosha*
2. The energy sheath, the *pranamaya kosha*
3. The mental sheath, the *manomaya kosha*
4. The wisdom sheath, the *vijnanamaya kosha*
5. The bliss sheath, the *anandamaya kosha*

Let's take a look at each in turn.

Characteristics of the Physical Sheath: Annamaya

The physical sheath consists of the physical body, which is sustained by food, air, and water. It is therefore called *annamaya,* the "sheath of food."

(*Anna* means "food" in Sanskrit, and *maya* means "magic" or "illusion.") We can nourish it through proper nutrition, hydration, and rest. When we do, we can become more attuned to the subtler sheaths.

To inventory the physical body, sit or stand upright. Feel your feet touching the floor or ground. Close your eyes, and notice the sensations within your body. Pay attention to what you feel. Can you feel your muscles and the weight of your bones on your seat or the bottoms of your feet touching the floor? Can you feel your heartbeat or hear its sound? By bringing your attention to your body, your awareness enters the physical dimension of your being.

Throughout the day, we can stop what we're doing to check our physical body. Just ask, "What sensations am I noticing?" The idea is simply to observe these feelings without attaching stories, labels, and judgments to them. This in itself is a form of dropping in.

Characteristics of the Energy Sheath: Pranamaya Kosha

This sheath is subtler than the physical sheath. As you may have noticed when playing with the energy between your hands (see exercise on page 35), the vital force known as prana produces subtle sensations in our bodies. Prana is what animates us physically. It appears when we are born and leaves when we die.

To be healthy and connected, we need to regulate our energy body. We do this through specific yogic breathing practices known as *pranayama*. When we consciously adjust our breathing patterns in certain ways, we can activate our PSNS or our SNS. We can also use breath to access the other subtle sheaths.

The seven energy centers known as chakras inhabit the *pranamaya kosha*. (We will explore these later in the chapter.)

To inventory your energy body, inhale through your nose and bring the air deep into your belly. Exhale very slowly. Feel the energy in and around you upon your exhalation, noticing as it pulses through your body. Can you feel tingling or rushes of movement? What about warmth? What do you perceive as you experience the sensations? Relax into feeling your breath entering and exiting your body as if you are being breathed—as if you are not the one doing the breathing. This is how you enter the dimension of your being that is your life force energy. More robust exercises are found later in this chapter.

Characteristics of the Mental Sheath: Manomaya Kosha

Mana means "mind" in Sanskrit. The mental body controls the way we process thoughts and emotions. It controls the physical body, the senses, and the brain and works in tandem with prana. The mind helps us survive and is the way in which we navigate our world. But when we are overreliant on the mind, we are subject to the machinations of the protective ego— our taskmaster of defense, rationalization, and judgment—and develop thought patterns that reflect our conditioned fears and anxieties.

The mental body is capable of so much more than this. As you have already learned and hopefully have been practicing, it can become the witness instead of being a reactive observer. Its well-being depends on the previous two sheaths. In other words, we need both a healthy physical body and a healthy energy body to have an optimally functioning mind!

To inventory your mental body, close your eyes and place your awareness in your head. Become aware of specific thoughts. Just notice them with curiosity. So much of our thinking is composed of habitual thought patterns. We have carved deep tracks in the brain from repeating certain thoughts over decades. Every thought shifts our biochemistry and emotional state. Ask if your thoughts are true. Ask if they are serving you. By becoming aware of your thoughts, you take the first step toward releasing the tight grip they have on you.

When you enter the dimension of your mental body, you can play around with thoughts to discover which ones are expansive and uplifting and which ones are constricting and "heavy." With practice, you can learn to shift this layer of awareness at will.

Characteristics of the Wisdom Sheath: Vijnanamaya Kosha

Vijnana means "knowing" in Sanskrit. Yogic philosophers have long taught that humans are distinguished from animals by this fourth sheath, which gives us the ability to possess wisdom. The wisdom body is a nonconscious dimension of awareness, which exists beyond the processing capacity of the thinking mind. Wisdom includes discernment, our ability to differentiate between what is and isn't useful and the capacity to make informed choices.

To enter the dimension of your wisdom body, simply become quiet and inquire as to what is true *right now*. This sheath is the home of our intuition, the part of us that just knows and gets "downloads" about what's right for us. The wisdom body offers insight. Listen to its truth.

The wisdom sheath can become distorted, however, when we over-identify with the ego mind. This can cause us great suffering. However, when we attune to our wisdom, we can establish a genuinely conscious approach. The traditional yogic system offers a comprehensive means of cultivating this sheath, including the set of ethical standards for self-discipline (the dos and don'ts) known as the *yamas* and *niyamas,* which encompass principles such as nonviolence, truthfulness, non-stealing, self-restraint, and non-covetousness.

Characteristics of the Bliss Sheath: Anandamaya Kosha

The subtlest sheath of our being, which is the one most connected to universal energy, is the bliss body, the *anandamaya kosha*. At its core sits the soul, the witness. To be aware of this dimension, we must enter a nonmental state in which we are simply being. Once we have accessed this awareness, we can perceive that we are both the observer and the observed, as all boundaries have dissolved. It is called bliss because this dimension feels amazing! But in this context, the definition of bliss extends far beyond one the human mind can grasp. Yogis believe that this bliss surpasses all understanding of the mind.

To enter the dimension of the bliss body, you need to become deeply relaxed and get out of the way of your thoughts by becoming aware of your own awareness. Feel your beating heart. Feel your energy pulsing through your body. Relax in stillness for as long as you can. Then notice the spontaneous release of joy and contentment. This can happen anytime, even in a small, everyday moment. Watch for it when you are walking down the street. Do you see the quality of light as it hits the trees and flowers? You may begin to notice things that have been there all along and observe everyday occurrences as they become moments of inspiration. Be present when it happens.

Connecting the *Koshas* to Leadership

Our leadership can benefit greatly from an appreciation and awareness of the fact that we are more than just our physical body and mind. Familiarity with the system of five *koshas* offers us a map for living and experimenting. We can learn to be more open to other ways of knowledge. We can have direct experience of the energy body and feel ourselves being connected to and guided by it. We can use our wisdom body to apply discernment to issues like ethical ways of living and working with others. Cultivation of the wisdom body is also important for leading an organization where there is often imperfect information combined with a need for rapid decision making.

Finally, for those who are truly interested in and committed to inner work, it is possible to experience the bliss body through a wide range of meditative practices. Leaders who learn to witness the activities and people around them in an unattached manner can bring true power and influence to the organizations they serve. Because they have cultivated their own presence, they can choose their response rather than reacting habitually. They are joyful in their activities and co-creative with others, thereby helping create cultures that are safe, healthy, and dynamic.

The Chakras: A Blueprint for Working with Our Energy as Leaders

As mentioned earlier, when we use not only our brain, but also our entire presence to lead, our abilities to perceive, process, digest, and respond are far more sensitive and accurate. The processing capabilities of the conscious mind are a small fraction of the processing capabilities of the entire body, which is organized and "wired" like a supercomputer.

In the yogic tradition, the energy body contains energy centers known as chakras. According to Ambika Wauters, psychotherapist and founder of the Institute for Life Energy Medicine, in *The Book of Chakras: Discover the Hidden Forces Within You,* "Try to imagine the chakras as a 'filtration system.' It purifies our energy from the gross, physical plane associated with our primal instincts and basic animal nature, turning it into the highly refined, spiritual plane that connects us with the source of life itself."[3] Many spiritual traditions describe the body this way—as a highly refined organ for processing information at multiple levels. The only distinction is that different systems use different vocabularies.[4]

The chakras offer a useful map for understanding the connection between energy and the physical body. The word chakra means "wheel" in Sanskrit. In yoga, it is understood that they constitute a convergence of energy fields. Although they are nonphysical and only exist in the *pranamaya kosha*, these vortexes of moving energy are key to our mental and physical health, as each organ system is located within a particular energy center.

Because the chakras store our emotions, memories, and traumas, when there is a blockage in an energy center that inhibits our ability to process information in its entirety, we can become ill. We typically only notice a blockage once it causes an issue in our physical or mental body.

In yoga, we try to understand where these blockages are so we can clear them. When we do, our amazing, complex processing system can work as an unfettered and integrated vehicle.

Let's take a quick look at the seven major chakras.

The Seven Major Chakra Centers

Energy is neither for nor against anything. Nuclear energy can provide enough electricity to illuminate a city or enough destructive force for a nuclear bomb. The energy itself is neutral—whether it is used to harm or to help is up to us. Each chakra has manifestations that represent either blockages or full expression—and in either case, the energy of that chakra's expression reflects the intentions of the user.

There are hundreds of chakras in the human body, but only seven main ones, which roughly correlate with the spine, starting at the tailbone and ending on the top of the head. The seven major chakras are each associated with a color.

Chakra 1: The Root Chakra

The root chakra is the first energy center in the body. Located at the base of the spine, it draws energy from the earth up through the feet and legs; from there it moves through the entire body. The root chakra grounds our beliefs and our connection to our tribe. It is about safety and security. It is the chakra of our survival. Its anatomical connections are the feet and tailbone. When this chakra is balanced, we are self-sufficient and responsible. When it is imbalanced, we may have issues with self-direction, survival, dependence, and anxiety. The associated color is red.

Chakra 2: The Sacral Chakra

The second chakra is located about three inches below the navel in the pelvic bowl. It connects us to our ability to enjoy life physically, including our sexuality. It is about relationships and emotions, expressing our needs, and giving and receiving. The emotional connection to desire is located here. Creativity and aliveness come from this chakra center, too. Its anatomical connections are to the spleen, kidneys, and reproductive organs. This chakra functions best when we care for and value ourselves. When it is imbalanced, we may experience issues with insecurities, fears of intimacy, and addictions. Its associated color is orange.

Chakra 3: The Solar Plexus Chakra

The third energy center is located slightly above the navel. It is considered our personal power center—the seat of our willpower and our physical and emotional vitality. Physical strength comes from metabolizing food and water, and the associated organs are those of the digestive system. This is also the source of our gut instinct, or the knowledge that comes from intuition. When this chakra is balanced and unblocked, we are confident and courageous. When it is stagnant and imbalanced, we may experience issues with self-sabotage, disempowerment, and apathy. Just as the energy from the sun animates all life on earth, the solar plexus chakra animates our endeavors. The associated color is yellow, like the powerful rays of the sun.

Chakra 4: The Heart Chakra

The heart chakra is found in the chest. The heart is the center of our energy system because it pumps the blood that circulates oxygen and other resources, keeping us alive. It serves to bridge the upper and lower energy centers and governs our empathy, love, and compassion. This chakra is associated with the heart and lungs, as well as the lymphatic and immune systems. When the heart chakra is balanced, we are open, loving, and compassionate with others. When blocked or imbalanced, we will have issues with compassion and trust. The associated color is green.

Chakra 5: The Throat Chakra

The throat chakra is anatomically connected to the throat, neck, mouth, teeth, and jaw. It governs our ability to express emotions and thoughts. When it is balanced, we are able to express ourselves through creative and articulate communication. When it is blocked, it prevents energy from rising from the lower chakras in the body, thereby preventing us from speaking our truth, trusting, being creative, or feeling motivated. The associated color is light blue.

Chakra 6: The Brow Chakra (aka the Third Eye)

The brow chakra sits between the eyebrows and about two inches behind the forehead. Energetically, it is associated with wisdom. Anatomically, it is connected to the endocrine and nervous systems. When the brow chakra is balanced, we can cultivate our intuition, discernment, and knowing, expanding our ability to see beyond our five physical senses. We can see the "big picture." When it is blocked or imbalanced, we may struggle with resilience, the ability to have a strong and independent mind, or intuition. The associated color is indigo.

Chakra 7: The Crown Chakra

The crown chakra is located on top of our head and connects us with higher consciousness. It is the opening for us to cultivate a connection to source energy. Through this center, we can gain a deeper understanding and self-realization that we are not separate from the whole of life. Instead, we are one with it. When this chakra opens, it reveals a deeper context and meaning for challenges and difficulties. We are no longer ruled by the ego—that divider and limiter. We have compassion and acceptance of life as it is and for ourselves as we are. When it is blocked or imbalanced, however, we may feel separated from the greater whole of existence. The associated color is violet.

Connecting the Chakras to Leadership

Leaders can benefit from cultivating awareness about the condition of our chakras and then taking steps to improve their balance. There are many resources to do this, including guided meditations. What's essential is to engage in a thoughtful exploration of how your chakras may be impacting you: your choices, actions, and physical ailments. When we are imbalanced, we will feel it in our bodies, and others can observe it in us.

The beginning of an investigation occurs when we are curious, inviting insights with the simple question, *Where, if anywhere, do I feel stagnant energy in my thoughts, body, or emotions?* If we notice blockages somewhere in our energy system, the body is harboring disease, or "dis-ease." Energetic "clogging" and stagnation prevent us from being able to fully process information and act in an integrated manner. When we can only use part of our capacity, we are vulnerable to ineffective decision making or action.

System Management: Your Breath Is the Key to Slowing and Harnessing Your Mind

To change our state of mind and our mood, the first step is to change the state of our breath. Breath is the single most important physiological action our bodies possess. We are hard-wired to prioritize breathing over everything else. We never really think of this because breathing happens automatically. We do not walk around worrying about how to breathe unless we are experiencing lung problems, including symptoms of asthma, COVID–19, pneumonia, emphysema, or seasonal allergies!

In addition to being our most powerful autonomous function, the breath can be trained to serve as the conscious connection between our autonomic nervous system (ANS) and our subconscious mind. Many of us have already experienced this. Many pregnant women are taught to use the Lamaze breathing technique during childbirth to stay present rather than become overwhelmed by intense waves of pain caused by uterine contractions.

Yoga takes this concept even further. It teaches that we can control our state of mind by controlling our breath. Is it possible to remain calm while hyperventilating during an active fight-or-flight response? Not really. When we feel threatened, our adrenaline and cortisol levels elevate to give us the energy to flee. In the office, when someone is coping with the pressure of a crisis situation, their voice is not as persuasive because their fear comes through in the pitch of their vocal tone.

Conversely, we can feel anxiety unwind when we inhale slowly through the nose while initiating the breath from our abdomen instead of the lungs and follow this up with an even longer exhalation through the mouth. Breathing in such a conscious and deliberate way is a powerful tool for shifting ourselves from reactors to responders and is the first step in presence.

How to Harness Your Mind Using Your Breath

When we inhale, we bring fresh oxygen into the body. When we exhale, we release carbon dioxide. When we inhale, we bring life force energy into our body. When we exhale, we expel metabolic products. When we inhale *actively*, we activate the SNS. When we exhale *slowly*, with *relaxation,* we activate the PSNS.

Most of the time, we want to slow down. Not only can slowing our breathing relax us and help us experience the present, but it can also bring us to a state of being present with *neutrality*. We can drop into a state of nondoing. This is the moment where we see what is as it is.

We can consciously use our breath to shift our bodies from a hypercharged, hyperventilating, sympathetically driven machine into a balanced one, where our natural healing capacities are allowed to flourish.

According to B.K.S. Iyengar, in *Light on Yoga:*

The chitta (mind, reason, and ego) is like a chariot yoked to a team of powerful horses. One of them is prana (breath), the other is vasana (desire). The chariot moves in the direction of the more powerful animal. If breath prevails, the desires are controlled, the senses are held in check and the mind is stilled. If desire prevails, breath is in disarray and the mind is agitated and troubled. Therefore, the yogi masters the science of breath and by the regulation and control of breath, he controls the mind and stills its constant movement. In the practice of pranayama, the eyes are kept shut to prevent the mind from wandering. "When the prana and the manas (mind) have been absorbed, an undefinable joy ensues." (Hatha Yoga Pradipika, chapter IV, verse 30)[5]

Karl, a COO, shared the following: "I am learning that regulating my state is all about how I utilize my awareness and my energy. Because I now practice taking five slow breaths at intervals throughout the day, I am able to remain in the present and be at peace without expectation. Not one day goes by that something doesn't hurt me. Now I don't dwell on it all day. I say, 'I breathe,' and I am at peace. In tough situations, I see that I cannot escape reality, but I can escape being in the past or the future."

Breathing Practices to Regulate Your State

There are a variety of breathing practices in yoga that can assist us. These *pranayama* ought to be practiced 10 to 15 minutes daily. Do them sitting with your back absolutely erect, from the base of your spine to your neck, and your chin perpendicular to the floor. The rest of your body should be relaxed, with no strain. They also should be done on an empty stomach. Eyes should be closed.

EXERCISE 5: **Alternate Nostril Breathing (*Nadi Shodhana Pranayama*)**

One of the most commonly used and recommended breath practices, suitable for most people, is alternate nostril breathing, or *nadi shodhana pranayama*. Its purpose is to balance the left and right hemispheres of the brain. This helps us access deeper capacities, settle the nerves, and quiet the mind. A *nadi* is an energy channel, while *sodhana* is the Sanskrit term for the act of purifying or cleansing. So you could say this technique purifies the nerves. You may find it helpful for reducing anxiety and racing thoughts. Try it before meditation or bedtime. It is also useful for gathering your energy and centering yourself as you transition between activities.

In this practice, we alternate between the right and left nostrils as we inhale and exhale, regulating the flow of air through our nasal passages. As we do, the activity of the mind becomes still.

Caution: People with medical conditions that affect the lungs, such as asthma or COPD, should consult a physician before trying this practice. If you feel any shortness of breath while doing it, stop immediately and let your breathing return to normal.

Here's how to do it.

EXERCISE 5: **Alternate Nostril Breathing (*Nadi Shodhana Pranayama*), cont.**

1. Raise your right hand to your face. Close the right nostril with your thumb and place your ring finger over the left nostril. Place your second and third fingers between your eyebrows to rest.

2. Lift your ring finger. Inhale through the left nostril, slowly, steadily, and deeply, fully filling the lungs. Retain the air for a moment.

3. Now gently press down on the outside of the left nostril again with your ring finger and then release your thumb from the right nostril. Exhale slowly.

4. Next, inhale through the right nostril, keeping the left nostril closed. Hold the air.

5. Gently press your thumb on the outside of the right nostril and then release your ring finger. Exhale slowly. This completes one entire cycle.

6. Repeat the sequence for 8 to 10 cycles.

7. Finish the practice by lying down on your back, closing your eyes, with blanket under neck and knees, if desired. It is essential to do whatever you need to in order to be able to fully relax. This is known as "corpse pose" (savasana). Remain in this pose for five minutes to fully integrate the changes it has produced.

EXERCISE 6: **Ocean Breathing (*Ujjayi Pranayama*)**

Ocean breathing is an extremely simple breath practice that immediately produces calm. Yogis use this technique to focus their minds while they're holding poses. It's a bit noisy, sounding sort of like Darth Vader breathing inside his helmet, so it would not be suitable during a meeting, but it can help improve concentration if you are feeling distracted.

There are no contraindications for ocean breathing. But if you have a stuffy nose or sore throat, you might find its sensations uncomfortable.

Here's how to do it.

1. Inhale through the nose and exhale slowly through the mouth for a few breaths, making the sound of "ha" during exhalation.

2. Now close your mouth, and both inhale and then exhale through the nose, still making the same sound, only with your mouth closed. Direct the movement of air to the back of your mouth, where the sinus passages meet the throat.

EXERCISE 7: **Skull Shining Breath (*Kapalabhati Pranayama*)**

This breathing technique is energizing and activates the SNS. It is not recommended when you are feeling stressed or in chronic overdrive, but it is helpful on days when your brain is foggy or you feel tired and need a pick-me-up. In breath work, it is the equivalent of drinking a cup of coffee, so do it once to become alert and then move on.

Caution: People with high blood pressure or heart conditions should not attempt skull shining breathing unless they are on medication and their blood pressure is well-regulated and in the normal range. They should consult their physician before doing so.

Here's how to do it. The key is the emphasis you place on your *out breath*.

1. Take a breath through your nose with a full, deep inhalation and a *long, slow* exhalation. On your next round of breathing, you can pick up the pace.

2. Begin pulling in your lower abdomen to force air out of your nostrils in short spurts. Keep your mouth closed and your face relaxed.

3. There is no need to inhale actively. Each inhalation will be passive and happen naturally. At this point, the breaths in and out become even in length and rapid-fire.

4. Continue for 60 to 90 exhalations. Then let your breathing return to normal.

5. Inhale deeply and hold as long as you can without struggle.

6. As you feel the rush of energy to your third eye, while holding your breath, tilt your head back with your nose pointed toward the ceiling. Hold your breath for as long as you can without strain.

7. As you exhale, relax your head back into a neutral, horizontal position.

8. Enjoy the moment between inhalation and exhalation.

9. You have entered a balanced state where you can become the witness.

10. Whenever you feel the urge to breathe, allow your breathing to return to normal.

The Practice of Dropping In

Dropping in is not just "slowing down" or "speeding up." It is about opening a portal to higher consciousness through the subtlest sheath of your being—the bliss body.

The Benefits of Dropping In

Dropping in has numerous benefits for leaders. Here are a handful:

- *It helps us change our state of mind.* We need good knowledge and good practices. Good knowledge is understanding that the mind can trick us into believing things. Good practice is dropping in. With this technique, we can change our state of mind easily. We only need to learn how to use our breath to access our body's relaxed natural energy.
- *It helps us access the witness consciousness.* When we breathe consciously, we engage in an experience in which we feel sensation and awareness. We become a neutral observer, someone who has full access to a field of possibilities.
- *It soothes our emotions.* Here, in his own words, is a CEO's summary of how practicing dropping in affected him as a leader: "I was spending most of my time at work in a state of anger, worry, and fear. You could read it in the air around me. My mental 'tapes' were so old—basically, I was still reacting to the authority my father had over me when I was a child. Although fear is endemic in every entrepreneurial venture, I was riding the fear train. Of all the techniques, dropping in produced the most noticeable changes for me. It revealed my subconscious to me, and I now realize there is nothing to fear."
- *It frees us from external distractions.* When we drop in, we can pay attention to pure sensation for its own sake, helping us break conditioned patterns of thought, feeling, and behavior. Our internal energy system is "hooked up," so we notice an aliveness, often manifesting as a feeling of warmth or as pulsing, throbbing, or tingling sensations. This is the language of the *pranamaya kosha.*

■ *It helps us recognize that a problem is within us rather than outside us.* We stop trying to fix others and instead focus on what is genuinely within our control: managing our internal energy and where we place our attention. When we drop in, we amplify our powers of self-observation. We are no longer seeing through the distorted lens of an unhappy memory or future anxiety.

■ *It gives us access to a massive supply of information, creativity, and energy.* Once we use breathing skills to shift our perspective, our leadership capacities radically expand as well.

■ *It enables us to consciously create our future.* A colleague commented to me about one CEO with whom I had been working: "His progress is jaw-dropping. It appears he has lost all reactivity and irritability. He has a Zen-like state. As he has learned to direct his breath in a new, competent way, he creates a safe environment. All the while, he is going through one of the biggest challenges of his life. There is a gentleness about him now. Previously, I've had interactions with him when he would declare victimhood. He would project disappointment and judgment of others. He has now entered the state of a master. It's a dramatic change."

■ *It is incredibly pleasurable and peaceful, and therefore, it is healing.* When we disconnect from our stressful and unhealthy habitual responses, our body can return to its natural homeostasis. This state of calm permits the body to naturally heal itself.

LEADERSHIP IN ACTION
How Dropping In Saved Sandra from Dropping the Ball

Consider Sandra, a former senior executive in a large company who left to start a company of her own. Sandra was extremely clear about her vision for her new company as well as the value proposition it would be offering to consumers. Having worked only in large-scale organizations, she found herself highly challenged by her new role as a startup CEO. Fear, therefore, was an understandable reaction.

But left unchecked, fear leads to indecision or ineffective action. One of the biggest responsibilities in my work with Sandra was to help her stay centered so that she did not retreat from her own greatness out of fear.

On one of our calls, she shared how frustrated she was with some of her investors, who had committed to large sums of money, and yet none of it had appeared. I began asking some questions to find out more about how she was communicating with them. She discovered that she expected from others that which she could not imagine herself because she was not centered. Because she couldn't create it in her own mind, she couldn't clearly communicate to others and therefore wasn't able to obtain the necessary funding.

Our work together focused on increasing her awareness by dropping in. We practiced the sensation of dropping in together. As we did so, she immediately recognized what her expectations were and saw that she needed to create the right conditions within herself first, so that she could achieve her desired outcomes.

Together we went through a brief exercise so she could center herself, and then we did a role-play, in which I was the other party in the communication. It usually takes a number of run-throughs before the body and brain absorb the lesson.

On the third try she had an epiphany: "I got it. I see what I wasn't doing." She engaged herself differently by dropping in, allowing her to focus on changing her own patterns, instead of the other person's. She was able to work within the only true circle of influence we have—the one within ourselves. The next day she let me know: "I just got the first $50,000, and $100,000 is coming in on Wednesday!"

This is just one of many similar experiences my client leaders have had in which dropping in has made a significant impact. It is important to note, however, that dropping in isn't a one-and-done event. It's an ongoing process of remembering to connect to our own energy and become present.

Dropping In Is Different from Mindfulness

Dropping in is not the same thing as mindfulness. When you drop in, you are mindful, but when you are mindful, you may not necessarily be dropped in.

Mindfulness simply means "having a heightened state of awareness." You can mindfully put your attention on pouring a cup of coffee in the morning. You are not necessarily dropped in while pouring the coffee because, if you were, you might not be able to pour it well!

Mindfulness is also not the same thing as being in a meditative state of energetic attunement. When dropped in, we are attuned to the frequency of our soul and connected to the universal energy of the field around us. When we are mindful, we are focusing on a single thing, but we may or may not be energetically attuned at all.

Dropping in is actually *mindless.* We empty the mind and attune to our sensations without labeling them, fully absorbed in our direct experience without necessarily having any focus at all. We are seeing what is, *exactly as it is,* and feeling pure sensations without the filters of the mind. This is a state of "choiceless awareness" where we are not thinking, labeling, or judging.

Once we are dropped in, we have left the valley of the ego mind and its distortions for the open field of neutrality.

Sometimes we drop in spontaneously, too. You have probably already experienced dropping in when you were practicing letting go in the last chapter. It is also an element in the practice of *yoga nidra,* or "yogic sleep," which you'll learn about in Chapter 5, "Integrate."

The Best Time to Practice Dropping In

Does your morning routine incorporate a conscious way to enter your day? As we discussed earlier, many leaders start their days reactively, without a specific practice for conscious connection to their presence. This signals the brain to run through its familiar circuitry, looking for problems to solve. And it will find them! While doing this, it is conjuring up all sorts of emotions and sensations in the body. A recollection of a disagreement with a co-worker may summon up frustration and tension in the jaw or knots in the stomach. We are off and running—but not in the desired forward direction. We are running quickly in circles, going nowhere. Our programs are actually running us!

Fortunately, there is a way out that requires no investment of money—only time, intention, and willpower. As with any habit, repetition is needed to solidify new neural wiring. One of the ways to make this practice easier is to work with the body's natural rhythms. The moments after we wake up are the best time to do any practices that connect the subconscious mind to our inner presence because our brain waves and circuitry are most receptive to change before we have been activated by external stimuli.

What we do in those moments sets the tone for the rest of the day. Our practice at this time can make all the difference in how we think, feel, and behave. Dropping in can be done at other times of the day as well, but the morning is particularly beneficial—and the closer to sunrise the better (although there is benefit any time of day). The best part is that we *can* control how we feel at the beginning of the day and choose to take actions that increase our presence, setting ourselves up to create what we truly desire.

The Dropping In Practice

Sit quietly someplace where you won't be distracted. The idea is to make yourself comfortable enough to stay in one position without movement. Position yourself with your sit bones on the edge of your chair and allow your spine to be upright so that you are open to the flow of your natural energy. Then, importantly, invite your body to "stay," as if you were training a puppy.

Be gentle and patient for a few minutes as you settle in and set an intention to create time for yourself and your body. Say this in the present tense: "I am kind to myself and to others" or "I connect within before speaking to others" or "I am patient."

Next, close your eyes to withdraw from the outer world and focus your attention inward. Focus initially on your breath. Just notice the pattern of your breathing with curiosity. Is it fast or slow? Heavy or light? Is it initiating from the top of your lungs or from your belly? Simply notice where you are right now without trying to change anything.

As you continue your inhale and exhale slowly and deeply, you will become increasingly relaxed. You are activating the PSNS by shifting your breathing pattern from that of inhaling rapidly from your upper lungs, thereby stimulating fight or flight, to breathing slowly from your abdomen, stimulating rest and digest. Such a breathing pattern helps us shift from living in a chronic state maintained by the SNS to one that is in balance.

By getting in touch with your sensations while experiencing relaxation, you move from a state of hypervigilance filled with fears and anxieties to an acute awareness of the present moment. The breath lives here. You are conscious and aware of the now, having left your conditioned mind and entered the domain of relaxation and access to your higher intelligences—wisdom, intuition, insight, and universal consciousness.

Here is the key thing to know about it: *It activates the third eye.* Dropping in happens most easily during a formalized breathing practice. In yogic breathing, there are two special moments where we pause the cycle of breath. One is after the exhale and just before the inhale, and the other is just after the inhale and prior to the exhale. At first the pause is just for a split second, but with practice this time can be extended.

In this space, we neither need to inhale nor exhale. The body is neither for nor against breathing in or breathing out. Now we can place all our attention on the spot between and slightly behind your eyebrows—the third eye. Here we are dropped in—plunged into the effortless space between our thoughts. Time stops. Doing stops. We do not judge our thoughts.

Just feel what you feel.

When your entire being is focused on the third eye in this moment, you effortlessly enter a state of neutrality. You are relaxed and centered. You are acutely aware of sensations as you feel them because you are fully absorbed in them. Your thoughts have receded to the background and no longer capture your attention. The breath modulation facilitates a responsive, peaceful state of presence.

Dropping into this breath gap allows you to experience the narrow space between thoughts when you become the observer. This is the link between the conscious and subconscious minds, the mechanism with which to break conditioned patterns derived from the past.

This is the clearest moment we have in which to observe what is as it is and become the nonreactive witness. When we are conscious, awake, and dropped in, we have disengaged from reactive patterns and experience relief from the past and future. We enter into the present moment, then the next moment, and then the next one after that. This is the state in which we have access to higher realms of creativity, synthetic thinking, and innovation. We disconnect from the ego mind, no longer focusing exclusively on what we want. When we are the witness, we can use *all* our human capacities to assimilate information, process or digest it, and respond to what is happening as it is taking place.

When we drop in, we access the state where everything we desire is possible.

CHAPTER 5

Integrate
Live with Intention

If the doors of perception were cleansed every thing
would appear to man as it is: Infinite.[1]

—WILLIAM BLAKE

Integration is more than a state of mind. It's a state of being. We know it when we feel it—and whenever we do, it enables us to go out to meet the world in a coherent, intentional manner.

How can we recognize it? As integrated beings with intentionality, we are:

- Relaxed
- Open
- Balanced
- Feeling
- Inspired
- Responsive
- Curious
- Present

When integrated, we notice our reactions, our thoughts, our language. We become the observer as much as the observed. We feel grounded and whole. Through integration, we release ourselves from the paralysis and stress caused by reactivity and are then able to direct the energy previously used to maintain tension in the body and mind toward healing and balance. We can now manage the strategy and operations of our business.

Integration allows the body to regulate itself effectively, responding to events as needed across the full range of sympathetic-parasympathetic polarity to restore its homeostasis. In a business context, this usually means we don't get stuck in chronic hyperdrive. Sure, we can gear up. But then we recover.

Have you ever noticed how, when a deadline is looming or a product launch is imminent, it can seem as if time is constricting? Integration creates a sense of grounded relaxation in us that seems almost to expand time, though what's really happening is a shift in perception, along with a reenergizing of our condition.

Because our energy is balanced and fully available when we are in an integrated state of being, inspiration visits more frequently and can actually take root. As we are also observing life without attachment, we can respond to what is present instead of reacting with habitual patterns of thought and feeling. From this, we gain clarity. Integration allows enough room in our hearts and minds for innovation and creative exploration to occur.

Leaders who are not integrated struggle to connect to others. It simply is not possible. When leaders are disconnected from themselves, the probability of inspiring co-workers and employees to find their own creative solutions in the workplace is greatly diminished. From your perspective, this would be like inviting people to dial into a specific radio frequency while you keep changing the bandwidth you're broadcasting on—and then wondering why they're getting garbled reception from you!

Tuning in to our personal frequency through integration lays a foundation for effective connection and communication, and thus effective co-creation, both as human beings and as leaders.

What Is Integration?

According to *Merriam-Webster* dictionary, the primary definition of the verb *integrate* is "to form, coordinate, or blend into a unified whole."[2] For our purposes, I am using it to mean the unifying of body, mind, and heart so that *all* our faculties are fully available to us. To integrate in a yogic framework, we need access not only to a calm mind, but also to our entire bodily field of awareness as we store all feelings, beliefs, and memories— everything that we are *not*—in the body. True integration occurs when we intentionally incorporate inputs from not only our mental constructs, but also from all our chakras and *koshas*.

Great leadership integrates centered mental strength with clear hearts, intuition, and courage.

What stops us from becoming integrated by thinking alone? The mind's self-protective mechanisms. We cannot use the mind to solve problems created by the mind! As we discussed earlier, the rational mind stores memories that prompt trauma and reactivity in the tissues of the body, where it can only speak to us through sensation, not in words. To integrate this stored information, we have to *transcend* the rational mind, which we do by activating the PSNS with intentional breathing. As we focus on breathing slowly and deeply, the mind is automatically calmed.

From here, we can enter into the yogic state of withdrawal, *pratyahara*. Then we apply our good knowledge, inward focus, clear intention, and observational skills and begin to notice that the body is speaking to us in the language of pure sensation, released through our energy body. It is always there, but now we are stopping long enough to notice it and "hear" (experience) what it is saying.

In the West, we are generally taught that the ANS, with its involuntary functions like heartbeat, digestion, body temperature, and breathing, is supposed to work in the background to maintain the body, so that we can use our mind independently. We view these involuntary systems as subservient to the brain, and most people never associate the body with the subconscious mind or with our intuition and creativity. Rather, these life-sustaining activities are considered "lower functions."

Yogic philosophy, however, has expounded for thousands of years that all levels of our being are involved in our intelligence. The yogis believe there is no distinction between our "lower" and "higher" selves, and that all parts of us are accessible and participate in everything we do.

In addition, yogic philosophy draws parallels between the intelligence of each individual and the intelligence that animates the universe. Each of us is understood to undergo the same repeating cycle of creation, preservation, transformation, and destruction as the entire cosmos, and to have the capacity to access the field of universal intelligence and infinite potential through the bodily sensations of prana we can feel running through us.

This is in contrast to Western beliefs that say there is a clear and predictable chain of cause and effect everywhere we look. Classical physics, formulated in the 17th century by Sir Isaac Newton to describe the movement of physical objects, informs us that for every action there is an equal and opposite reaction. This is known as the *third law of motion.*[3]

Yogic philosophy is more aligned with quantum physics, a field of study devised in the late 1800s and early 1900s to explain the behavior of the universal energy that underlies material reality. From a quantum view, uncertainty is part of every moment and action. It also recognizes that the act of observation often shifts the results that the observer sees. Perhaps most significant to our exploration of leadership in this book is that when it comes to the field of quantum energy interpenetrating our physical world, solid material particles and nonmaterial energy—with its uncertainty—have been proven to coexist.

Everything material is also energy.

We are energy beings.

Extrapolated to the social perspective, the idea that there is no separation on the level of our quantum energy implies that what happens within a single individual can impact a larger unit, whether that's a family or a whole culture. A leader's internal state affects everyone throughout the entire organization.

Ideally, individual leaders who are integrated within themselves would create integrated teams in turn that are well-suited to tackle the enormity of business and societal challenges in this turbulent era. The complexity of our 21st-century challenges has created a novel business paradigm that emphasizes collective/team leadership more than individual performance. Yet our personal integration as leaders is the key to unlocking our highest capacity on behalf of our families, colleagues, employees, organizations, communities, and world.

The Power of Embodied Knowledge

When we're feeling stressed, most of us simply carry on as if we can suppress and manage all our difficulties on our own. The ego mind makes up all kinds of stories about our experiences, but the body reveals the truth. This is why checking in with the body is so important to the process of integration and why I consider techniques drawn from yoga so valuable. Knowing something intellectually and living it as a tangible experience are two dramatically different things.

Which can you do more easily right now: solve a geometry problem or ride a bike? No matter how long it's been since you've been on a bike, it likely would be much easier for you to hop on one and whisk away on it than it would be to tackle a geometry problem without refreshing your knowledge of certain formulas. The difference is that riding a bike is *embodied knowledge:* You kinesthetically learned the skill of adjusting your body weight and position to help you stay upright and balance. Doing geometry, on the other hand, is a purely mental activity. You probably learned it sitting still in a chair.

My point is that embodied knowledge is *felt*, and because we can feel it, we can easily remember it or re-create the experience on demand. The key to lasting integration is creating new neural patterns. The permanence of embodiment occurs through consistent, focused repetition. When we practice embodying our presencing skills frequently or daily, we reinforce the integration of everything we are learning so that when we need it, we can call on it quickly. Keep doing the exercises I've given you so far and you'll be rewarded. *Transformed.*

And it may interest you to know that the neurology that's changing with your practice isn't just in your head; it's resident throughout the body. Brain, gut, heart, eyes, and other areas of the body all have nerves and neurons that can be "wired" together. The human nervous system is a marvel!

Imagine going to the gym once a week to lift weights. You wouldn't accomplish much, would you? At this level of practice, your efforts would be limited to maintaining the strength and coordination you already have rather than enabling you to stretch, tone, and build more muscle. Likewise, practicing the new skills of presencing and leadership that I'm sharing in this book in frequent, short bursts is preferable to doing them only once a week.

To make real gains in integrating the skills of opening, letting go, and dropping in, more frequent repetition is needed. Start small, with the clear intention to move forward a bit each day. Challenge yourself to settle on consistent times to practice, such as once in the morning (not unlike brushing your teeth) or prior to entering a weekly staff meeting.

Also consider exploring role-playing after you've used an integration technique. In an integrated state, we can effectively prepare for something we wish to happen in a certain way, such as an important conversation. I often use this technique with clients (and for myself) who are getting ready to do something they find emotionally challenging, like giving a speech, negotiating a deal, terminating an employee, or running a group meeting. We increase the probability of an effective outcome when we have an embodied, integrated practice experience of an impending task. We can then re-create the sensations within our bodies when the time comes.

Perhaps the most important factor as you face your challenges is to have self-compassion. When we can tenderly hold space within ourselves for our difficult emotions, feelings, and memories, we are integrating them. The human experience is vast, diverse, and rich. Creation and destruction, joy and sadness, health and sickness are all a part of it. I have learned the importance of fostering self-compassion—both for knowing and believing that I am having a human experience, and that human experiences are often difficult and painful. Through self-compassion, my ability to remain integrated becomes easier.

Our challenges (and our responses) make up our humanity. Embodied knowledge of our whole self means we do not judge ourselves for being human or reject ourselves for what we are aware of. Our existence is enough. We simply *are*. We accept, honor, and acknowledge that others are having human experiences, too. As an integrated being, we can witness the human experience without judgment, denial, or shame. Acceptance of our whole self liberates us to focus on what we want to create and to declare a clear intention.

When breath is preceded by awareness and followed by self-compassion, we are on the way to integration. We have access to all our capacities.

LEADERSHIP IN ACTION

How Sandra Used Integration to Prepare for a Bold Career Move

The story of my client Sandra illustrates the concept of integration in a leader. She began working with me at a time of significant change in her life and career. She was working toward a number of goals, including, in her words, "Being able to access the full power of my body and emotions. As I enter the next stage of my career, I'd like to feel stronger in who I am."

After several months of helping Sandra learn the tools of dropping in, she reported that intentional breathing had become a cornerstone habit for her. Of this integrated skill, she said, "Through my breath work, I'm learning to let things happen vs. make things happen. I now see that my anxiety comes from feeling imbalanced by wanting to have both roots and wings."

Emotionally, for her, "having roots" meant feeling secure in her current role. "Having wings" meant being comfortable with, even enthusiastic about, exploring new possibilities.

As Sandra integrated her natural being into her decision making, she developed the will to take a big risk: leaving the safety of her senior-level role in a large organization to start a company of her own. The momentum began to build as she practiced integration.

Over a period of several months, Sandra practiced staying open and expressing curiosity about her inner landscape. In one of our meetings, she then confidently stated: "I see that work is about integration. Integration is also my personal theme for this career transition. I combine my personal life and my work life at a high level, and when I allow myself to integrate all these parts, I can take on more. When I'm integrated, I can see that anything is possible, including things that I haven't ever dared hope for until now.

"Practicing integration has made me happier. Someone who didn't have the same complexities in life as mine would not have come up with the business proposition for my company. I see now that I *am* my market. I *am* my customer. I *am* my company. With these new practices, as I reached toward integration regularly, things I formerly perceived as hurdles became assets."

Sandra's self-knowledge was strong, and her practices for opening and dropping in were securely established. As the company came into being, she dealt with many issues that were new to her as a leader. She noted, "I need to invest more time in emotional preparedness. I can no longer just barrel my way through work. When I take time to get clear, it benefits everyone.

"When I drop in, it helps me get things done. I can better prioritize. I can also teach others to empower and trust. As I get over the fears in myself, I overcome fears about the marketplace. I move forward boldly and confidently."

One year later, when I checked in with her on her state of being and its impact on her leadership, she noted: "When I'm centered and integrated, the rest of the team picks up on it. But when I turn myself inside out to be what people need, I go in all directions at the same time. In order for me to put myself out there as a leader, I have to be present to what is. It's not about catching up—it's about *leveling up*. The yogic skills you taught me help me to shift from focusing on my tactics to feeling thoughtful and inspired.

"What works is being centered and present with people. I can't be in the present moment when I'm worried about the future. If I haven't committed myself to this, I don't relax about what's ahead for me and the company. The only thing I can control is who I am going to be. I'm going to focus on that now. As things get tough, I see that I'm going to be and embody hope for the team. My job is to give the people I lead hope."

Integration Occurs When We Move from Thinking and Doing to Feeling and Being

I have found that nothing keeps me integrated as much as time on my yoga mat. For me, it is the felt experience of movement in the body reconnecting me to sensation that does the trick. When I lose the rhythm of my practice, my connection to myself can easily become disrupted. But if it does, I notice that I am becoming disintegrated and I know how to reconnect through various sequences of postures, breath work, and meditation. As I do yoga, it feels as if I am coming home. Although it has taken time for me to develop this practice, I look back on the effort I put into it as one of the most worthwhile endeavors of my life. And the practice is ongoing.

When energy channels in the body are unblocked, integration becomes possible. Yoga postures are useful tools to help clear the pathways through which energy flows, as are acupuncture and acupressure. There are also other energy medicine techniques, including Reiki, tai chi, and Jin Shin Jyutsu, that share the focus of helping us move away from the mental state of thought into observing energy and feeling its accompanying sensations in the body.

The breath also helps us form a connection to our awareness or consciousness. When we integrate through breathing, our prana is no longer trapped. We move from awareness of the physical act of breathing in and breathing out toward transformation beyond our past patterns. The mind releases its tension into the energy body, where it is transformed from reacting to witnessing. We are now neutral. We are in the present moment, experiencing it for all that it offers us without being held back by past distortions created by our habits of mind.

When we become captivated by sensations, we let go of who we are not so that we can see what is as it is. We move from duality (oriented toward separateness) to polarity (being integrated and dynamically balanced within ourselves) and then, ultimately, to experiencing unity with ourselves so we can bring it to others. We shift from orienting by the clock to having a sense of timelessness. When we do, we can see the distortions created by the mind pass by and through us, so that they no longer have the power to grip us. We are also given an opportunity to reprogram our mind to manifest new intentions.

All this is available to you and everyone else who desires it. I encourage you just to begin with a small step in the direction of integration. Notice for a few minutes each day what's happening for you physically, mentally, and emotionally, and then be patient. Watch how easily you become familiar with and desirous of the experience of integration. If you are thinking you don't have time to do this, don't fret; when it is right for you, the time will appear.

The Five Stages of Integration

There are five stages involved in integration. These are:

- *Observational awareness.* First, we become aware of our different states of mind and being. When we are still, we can observe these states moving through us and become more aware of how they affect our behaviors.

- *Unhooking.* We unplug from the habits of the mind that have been unconsciously created. We disidentify with them. We don't fight or feed them. Instead, we use our tools. For example, we could sit still, engage in a conscious breathing practice, dial in to the sensations in our body, and spend a few minutes relishing the calm. This gives us an opportunity to become an observer of our habits of mind instead of being victimized by our thinking. Letting go is a form of unhooking.

- *Setting conscious intentions.* Through integration practices like *yoga nidra* ("yogic sleep"), which is described at the end of the chapter, we begin using conscious thought and intention to design what we want to create. Our intentions are planted in the subconscious mind so they can take root and flourish during a state of deep relaxation. This requires us to be fully engaged—and interestingly, a relaxed, integrated state of being promotes full engagement.

Seeding our intentions in this way allows us to stay present and take actions consistent with what we want, enabling us to move forward in spite of any fears or doubts. If we work consistently on the same intention for a period, the changes in our behavior can be significant. Test this premise for yourself, and you will gain confidence in this method!

In setting an intention, we focus on the thing we desire. We therefore must use positive, expansive language. For example, in reflecting on your daily commute to the office, you might say, "My intention is to be a safe, alert, and mindful driver whenever I'm behind the wheel." We also avoid fear-based language because it energizes contraction. For example, you would not say, "I don't want to crash the new car."

Regarding your eating habits, you'd say, "I make healthy food choices that promote well-being in my body." You wouldn't say, "I don't want to be overweight anymore."

Receiving. When we receive and acknowledge others, there is an energetic exchange between the person who shares and the receiver. Harmony occurs when we are in a state of polarity, where our being and receiving are in balance with our giving and taking of action. Polarity is the state in which "flow" happens. Once we notice that we can simply allow rather than force things, our actions can flow from trusting our connection to the present moment.

Integrating. Integration allows all the disparate elements of our being to come together so that we can heal and create wholeness. This is the state in which our chronic holding patterns will finally be able to be "digested," "metabolized," and released spontaneously in ways we could not have previously imagined. Our attachments and need to judge, be right, or be in control soften. In this fully integrated state, we observe and allow. What we need to release simply leaves us, without effort. What needs to be embraced will enter, as we have created the fertile soil for new growth. Full integration with the field of energy allows manifestation to occur effortlessly.

As mentioned earlier, one of the most potent tools for effortless integration is a guided practice known as *yoga nidra*. The power of this technique comes from taking disparate energy found throughout the body and collecting it in the third eye (or sixth chakra), the energy center located in the center of the head, between the eyebrows. (More will be said about *yoga nidra* toward the end of the chapter.) The release of trapped energy from the third eye doesn't involve force or "doing." Knowing the landscape and the treasure that lies beneath the third eye makes it simple to diminish stress and heal the body.

With ongoing practice, the groundwork is laid to awaken our highest capacities.

Why Integration Is Central to Effective Leadership

Having a practice that leads to integration and intentional living has important benefits for leaders. Integration is an important step that allows a leader to become an observer instead of a reactor. It allows us to realize the sources of the expectations we put on others that prevent us from being present to people as they are now.

Integration is the precursor to conscious, resonant communication with others. Leaders who are integrated within themselves embody an intention, solve problems, and co-create in a way that achieves results, maintaining healthy relationships through trust and reducing conflict.

Integrated leaders have moved from relying solely on rational thought in their work to incorporating intuitive, creative insights and other nonlinear breakthroughs. They no longer focus exclusively on outcomes or believe that the ends justify the means; being in a connected relationship all along the way toward a mutually desired outcome enriches their daily life and fills their work experience with presence.

Equanimity: An Additional, Significant Benefit of Integration

When we are unable to metabolize the tension we feel, we react to perceptions in the present that are based on past memories. When we are integrated, our perceptions are exposed as mirages—artificial creations our minds project on the world around us that seem real. When we are integrated, we are inoculated against SNS hijacking.

When integrated, we can experience both our challenges and victories through a clear lens. We are not attached to goals or outcomes per se but can be joyful in whatever we are doing at every stage. Integration raises our capacity to maintain equanimity in difficult times. Our relationships reflect this strength and joyfulness. Integration also provides us with natural immunity from one of the most dreaded conditions of our time—chronic stress.

When Is It a Good Idea to Pause and Get Integrated?

Taking a few minutes to pull yourself together and set an intention is beneficial before any activity. Here are some ideas of when to use an integration technique. Add your own to this list as you discover them in the course of doing business and interacting with your team and other people. Initially, this may seem artificial, but soon you'll do it automatically because the skill will have become embodied knowledge. In time, you may be able to integrate at any moment if you notice yourself being pulled out of alignment.

Try integrating:

- *First thing in the morning.* Remember, even a brief morning practice can yield significant benefits. How we enter the day makes a difference in how we feel and how effective we are in accomplishing what matters most as the day unfolds.
- *Before and after a meeting or phone call.*
- *Transitioning between activities.*
- *If you notice you're falling apart emotionally.* As the number of activities, unexpected events, and disappointments piles up, we may reach a point during the day that we begin to feel like we're unraveling or disintegrating. If this happens, we need to stop and observe what is going on in our mind, body, and emotions to get reintegrated.
- *If you're distracted, doubtful, confused, or experiencing brain fog.* In this technological marvel of a world, most businesspeople are being stimulated all day long by beeping, chiming, ringing, flashing, and vibrating communication devices. The antidote to the cognitive drain they cause is silent inward focusing and realignment with our

energy and intention. By the way, many of our devices are designed to be addictive by triggering the release of tiny rushes of dopamine, a neurotransmitter involved with the pleasure and reward centers in our brains. Be mindful that this kind of stimulation may eventually lead to a temporary depletion that makes life feel a bit flat. When the temporary rush of a dopamine burst passes, the stuck energy remains and our capacity to achieve integration is diminished, not restored.

- *When you're suffering from decision fatigue.* Social psychologist Roy F. Baumeister coined the term "decision fatigue" that affects all of us. Even as we shop, we have an overabundance of choices in any given category. Leaders are being bombarded even more than the average person. We are more likely to fall into the trap of cognitive biases and habitual behavior if we're mentally exhausted.[4] Integration practices can give the brain a much-needed break.

- *When you are feeling "triggered."* Being triggered is when a past trauma or anxiety about the future comes alive for us in the present. As we saw in Chapter 3, "Let Go," any type of external stress that has this effect on us may be thought of as an edge. If we have practiced going to our edge consistently in a non-stressful situation, when we're "in the game" during the day, we can draw in our focus, breathe, and set an intention to shift from a stress-based response to an integrative, witness-based presence. There will be many opportunities to become triggered in our day. We must remember that when we become disintegrated, we may react with anger, frustration, or impulsivity regardless of how much we have practiced responding calmly.

One of the best times to step back and activate our practices is before we blow everything up due to trauma or fear by yelling or sabotage ourselves with hesitancy or unhealthy, self-soothing tactics, like eating junk food. When we notice that we're feeling triggered, we can choose to observe our initial reaction and let it pass so we can reintegrate.

Furthermore, I would advocate that rather than judging others for reacting, we accept them with gratitude because we have newfound abilities to choose a different way. Also, rather than judge another person or circumstance for triggering us, I suggest we thank them for revealing our reactive patterns to us. Every trigger can be recognized as blocked energy within us that needs to be liberated. By placing our attention in the third eye and bringing the energy to it, we can convert this blocked energy into released prana in an instant. The third eye helps us drop into the state of being the witness, from which we can simultaneously observe our potential reaction based on our history and choose a different response based on what is currently occurring. In so doing, we release our attachment to the trigger, and it gets digested by the body through the third eye rather than redeposited and stored. The choices we make afterward then determine our outcomes. Through gentle, consistent retraining, we learn how to return to integration when disintegration due to emotional upset happens during the day.

- *At the end of the day, before bedtime.* Good sleep hygiene requires that we downshift from the busyness of the day. Using a guided integration technique, such as *yoga nidra*, prior to hitting the sheets (or even while lying in bed, if you want) is great preparation for sleeping. Read about this in the section at the end of the chapter.

Ayurvedic Wisdom: The Yogic Art of Living

Integrated leaders aim to integrate all aspects of themselves. This includes lifestyle management: caring for the physical body through clean food and water, exercising, and other self-care habits that support wholeness. Integration more easily inhabits a body that is well-tended.

Although not a requirement for integration, you may be interested to explore the basic concepts of Ayurveda, the sister science to yoga, which is an entire field dedicated to the art of living. The word *Ayurveda* has two Sanskrit roots: *ayuh,* meaning "life," and *veda,* meaning "science" or "knowledge." This traditional Indian medical system, dating back more than 3,000 years to the Vedas, offers us a comprehensive methodology to integrate our being as individuals, as well as our person with the whole of nature and the life force energy. Ayurveda includes attunement to ingredients that are in harmony with the seasons and timing our food consumption according to our circadian rhythms, sleep routines, and exercise regimens that are conducive to an individual's constitution.

Ayurveda views health (*svastha*) as a state in which mind, body, and senses interact harmoniously. Its blueprint to wellness includes recognizing five basic elements of nature that are present in everything, including our bodies:

- Earth (*prithvi*)
- Water (*apas*)
- Fire (*agni*)
- Air or wind (*vayu*)
- Space or ether (*akasha*)

Furthermore, every substance is understood to contain all five of these elements in some ratio. That said, in a given substance, one or two elements typically are predominant over the others.

Just to give you some examples, a potato, a tuber that grows buried in the soil, contains the earth element. By comparison, an apple, a fruit that grows on a tree, contains the air element. The spice cumin, a powder ground from seeds, is a combination of the air and fire elements.

When it comes to the human body, there are three basic energies (*doshas*), which account for constitutional differences between people: *pitta*, *vata*, and *kapha*. The root of the term *dosha* is the Sanskrit word *dosa*, meaning "fault" or "disease." Each of us has traits and tendencies that are recognizably *pitta*, *vata*, and *kapha*. The energetic nature of *pitta* in terms of the five elements of nature defined by Vedic tradition is predominantly fire (*agni*) with some water (*apas*). The energetic nature of *vata* is a combination of air or wind (*vayu*) and space (*akasha*). The energetic quality of *kapha* is a combination of earth (*prithvi*) and water (*apas*).

The balance of the three *doshas* governs all physical and mental processes in our bodies and dictates how we should feed and care for them. Each energy can go awry in its own way—through deficiency or excess—and responds to counterbalancing interventions. Fire needs water to soothe its heat. Air, which is associated with movement, needs earth to ground it. And so on.

We are born with an innate and specific balance between the *doshas* that we maintain for our entire life span. While everybody contains elements of each, we typically have either one primary and one secondary *dosha* or just a primary one. When we live in harmony and maintain our natural balance, we thrive. But if we become physically and mentally imbalanced for any reason, we create the conditions for illness and dysfunction to arise.

An analogy would be the relation of firewood and a fire. If we throw a large log on a smoldering fire, it is unlikely to ignite. Instead, it will produce smoke and ash—and, as the wood will not burn fully, we'll also be creating waste. Likewise, sawdust is inappropriate fuel for a raging fire. Although it will create a flash and some brief additional heat, they cannot be sustained. A better option is to feed the low fire smaller sticks and build the embers until they can ignite a log and burn longer. Then adding a larger log will produce sustained heat.

Matching our food choices and lifestyles to our bodies follows similar principles. To flourish physically, emotionally, and mentally, we need to know how to match our life choices to the needs of our bodies. The foods we eat may either pacify or aggravate our particular *dosha*. If a person with a *pitta dosha* eats highly spicy food, that will aggravate their internal fire. Similarly, if they eat foods that are cooling, this will pacify the tendencies of their constitution toward fire. Certain spices and foods aggravate or pacify *vata* and *kapha doshas* as well.

This doesn't necessarily mean we have to entirely ban certain types of food from our diet—we just don't want to overdo aggravating foods. It is helpful to consider the 80/20 rule. If at least 80 percent of the foods we consume are *dosha*-friendly, up to 20 percent could be otherwise.

Let's take a closer look at how the three *doshas* show up in our constitutions.

- *Pitta.* In brief, *pitta* is characteristically oily, sharp, hot, light, moving, liquid, and acidic. A *pitta*-dominant person is typically goal-oriented, of muscular build, and has good digestion. When balanced, a *pitta* leader expresses courage, drive, and intellect. They have stamina and enjoy working and collaborating. When imbalanced, this leader can be edgy and irritable and display ego, and they may experience inflammatory diseases, like heartburn and rashes. Anecdotally, I have observed that many successful executives are *pitta* dominant.

- *Vata.* In brief, *vata* is characteristically dry, rough, light, cold, subtle, and mobile. A *vata*-dominant individual is typically quick thinking, thin, and fast-moving. When balanced, a *vata* leader is active, creative, and gifted, with a natural ability to communicate. When imbalanced, this type shows anxiety and may develop dry skin and constipation.

- *Kapha.* In brief, *kapha* is characteristically moist, cold, heavy, dull, soft, sticky, and static. A *kapha*-dominant person typically has a solid body frame and a calm temperament. When balanced, a *kapha* leader is often blessed with naturally good health, endurance, and mental peace. When imbalanced, the body of this type can become weighed down with fluids, leading to sinus congestion or obesity. Mentally, an imbalanced *kapha* may become lethargic or depressed and stubborn.

According to Ayurveda, we are most susceptible to imbalances in our primary *doshas*. Like is understood to increase like, while opposites increase balance. Therefore, a *vata* person who is exposed to cold, dry air; raw food; and constant stimulation will become excessively *vata* and imbalanced. They do better consuming warm, moist foods like oatmeal, soups, and cooked vegetables. A *pitta* person who eats spicy or sour food and overworks will become imbalanced with inflammation. *Pitta* does better with cooling foods, like cucumbers and melons, and avoiding red meat. A *kapha* person benefits from eating pungent, bitter, and astringent foods; avoiding red meat and dairy; and eating a lot of greens, including bitter and astringent vegetables.

In the Resources section, I offer suggestions for where to learn more about the *doshas* and how to build an appropriate lifestyle to keep yours in balance.

20 Complementary Qualities of Experience to Balance

Ayurveda identifies 20 qualities (*gunas*) that can be used to describe every substance or experience. Because Ayurveda focuses on harmony that requires the balance of opposites, these qualities are organized into the following 10 pairs (see Figure 5.1 on page 119).

FIGURE 5.1: **Ayurveda Pairings**

Heavy	Light
Slow/dull	Sharp/penetrating
Cold	Hot
Oily	Dry
Smooth	Rough
Dense	Liquid
Soft	Hard
Stable	Mobile
Gross	Subtle
Cloudy/sticky	Clear

These qualities are important for understanding our basic nature and how to bring it into balance for the sake of our wellness, creativity, and joy. For example, during the winter (a cold, dry season), people with *vata dosha* benefit from warm, oily foods to balance the *vata*-aggravating weather. The *vata dosha*, characterized by motion and change, also requires predictable routines. This is especially important during a season where there is much wind and movement (typically in autumn) so as not to increase the dominance of air and space.

Conversely, in summer, a hot and humid season, we want to eat light, cold foods to counterbalance the *pitta*-aggravating weather. The *pitta dosha* requires calming activities, such as tai chi, walking, yoga, or swimming.

Many of us in the West are engaged in doing exactly the opposite of what will bring our bodies' natural constitutions into harmony. Particularly in the business world, many of the most successful individuals seem to have *pitta* constitutions. But the stress, coffee, lack of sleep, unpredictable eating schedule, and other lifestyle factors aggravate rather than restore our balance if we are *pitta*-dominant.

Even if we are not constitutionally *pitta* (or *vata* or *kapha*), we can develop a *pitta* (or *vata* or *kapha*) imbalance under the right conditions.

Understanding a bit of Ayurvedic wisdom helps to explain the vast number of health and stress-related symptoms experienced by leaders. As previously discussed, a disturbance in one *kosha* affects the others. Similarly, a disturbance in our energy body may eventually manifest as disease. As you work on integration, you will become more cognizant of areas in your life that need to be brought into balance.

Managing our lifestyle and nutrition strengthens our physical body so that we have access to all our energies and capacities as leaders. Ayurveda offers a blueprint for this.

Taking Integration Forward

To maintain integration, we need to move from practice to consistent application in our daily work and lives. When we do, we notice that our relationships with others are now harmonious. We can connect our hearts and minds with our intentions and co-create with others. We are now integrated with ourselves and therefore ready to connect with others.

Yoga Nidra: The Sleep of the Yogis

Although deep brain waves are usually reached while awake only by the most experienced meditators, there is a helpful shortcut to reach this state: *yoga nidra,* the "sleep of yoga." This simple yet effective guided practice can afford anyone access to these deep brain wave states while awake and lying down. It is not necessary to spend 25 years and thousands of hours in meditation to enjoy its benefits. *Yoga nidra* can be done in as little as 30 minutes and without any previous training or experience; the average guided session could last up to an hour. Consider it a brain hack! (See Resources for recommendations of guided *yoga nidra* audios and videos.)

Yoga nidra helps us remain balanced in the polarity of the universe, which is composed of pairs of opposites, like feminine and masculine, yin and yang, and positive and negative magnetic fields. The Ayurvedic complementary qualities describe polarities, too.

As we go through life, we pick up conditioning from every experience. We develop the likes and dislikes that shape our preferences. Cognitively, we judge others and ourselves. We take stands either for or against things. These preferences for duality separate us from our true nature of polarity, the energy of the entire field that is expressing itself through us, in which we are present and integrated.

Duality is the for/against posture we sometimes take in life that separates us from ourselves and from others. When we live in a state of duality, we experience tension, always trying to work our way back to what "feels better," in accordance with our past conditioning. The ego, which is always ready to fight for survival, drives this way of being.

In addition to creating ongoing tension, living in a persistent state of duality creates stress and disease in our bodies. We are unable to tolerate uncomfortable feelings, and we see the solution as doing, doing, and doing even more. We become addicted to busyness and live in sympathetic overdrive. We avoid introspection and silence, soothing ourselves with devices and substances that distract us from simply feeling our emotions. When we live this way, we accumulate stress. Our negative emotions—the reactive ones, including fear, anger, jealousy, and anxiety—reside here.

If we constantly react and operate from a hyper-aroused SNS, these states become chronic and habitual, robbing us of the natural healing power of our balanced energy. Without rebalancing with the relaxation of the PSNS, our energy is drained. We create ongoing stress and disease.

Living in duality makes us unable to experience the body's natural state of well-being. Without getting to the root of why we are imbalanced in the first place, we experience suffering and cannot heal. The best we can hope for is a short-term bandage, something to cover the wound. For deeper healing to occur, our body must return to polarity, our homeostatic state. *Yoga nidra* is one vehicle that can take us there.

During sleep, our brain waves progressively slow down. These brain wave states of deep sleep restore the body. However, conflict, stress, and conditioned mental and emotional reactions do not get cognitively processed and chemically metabolized when we sleep. So we may wake up in the morning feeling less tired (although many people do not), but our patterns of reactivity are still there.

Yoga nidra restores the state of polarity because it enables us to enter the subconscious energy body (the *pranamaya kosha)* while we are awake.

As we relax, we set an intention simply to let everything be, and then the body's natural energetic healing processes take place. We move from a state of duality to a state of polarity with no effort on our part.

Yoga nidra is based on the yogic philosophy that we exist in the multiple levels of being—our five *koshas*—all at once, even those levels we are not consciously aware of. Our perceptions tend to rely on identification with our mind *as if* it is our entire body, or with just the physical structures of the body, while ignoring the other levels of our being. When we connect to the sensations in our body as pure sensations, without identifying with them or labeling them, we are actually accessing the universal intelligence that allows us to function as more present. And this is what *yoga nidra* helps us do.

Yoga nidra is a magical state because while we do it, we are awake. The mind is gently engaged, yet not doing. If I haven't yet stated it clearly enough, *yoga nidra* is *guided.* Another person is reading instructions (often on a recording) while we lie supine and listen to them.

What makes *yoga nidra* unique is that we are completely aware of all that is taking place within us and around us, yet we are entering the states associated with our deepest brain waves—theta and delta states. Theta brain waves can be seen during hypnosis and trance states. Research has linked them to memory formation. Delta waves are slow and low, like a drumbeat. Theta waves first appear in light sleep, and delta waves persist into deep sleep. These waves stimulate healing and regeneration.

Yogis believe that the *yoga nidra* technique offers the opportunity to move through multiple levels of consciousness while observing the subconscious mind, thereby becoming more self-aware. Not only is the body restored and reset, but we can also eliminate subconscious conflicts and conditioning at the root.

We begin by self-describing an intention that is simple, short, and in the present tense. For example, "I am a connected, present listener with others." This is a commitment we make to support what we desire and remind us of our true nature. In this way, we prepare the soil of our brain for the implantation of our desires.

When an intention is planted at the beginning of the *yoga nidra*, the deep relaxation and altered brain waves allow it to easily take root in the subconscious layer so that it can manifest. *Yoga nidra* also helps uproot the weeds embedded within us that distort our perceptions, restricting us to our past conditioning instead of allowing us to stay in the present. In doing so, *yoga nidra* offers more than a technique—it is a place in which we can awaken that which is dormant within us. We plant the garden of our dreams and allow it to bloom.

Yoga nidra can be a wonderful experience of intuitively dreaming our goals into existence and support our waking actions.

Through *yoga nidra*, we learn to easily enter the space in which our complementary opposites are truly balanced. Instead of repeating the infinite cycle of stress caused by overreliance on the SNS and seeking to restore balance through substances, we break the pattern. We enter into a new relationship with our body, one in which our *natural* energy is expressed and restored in a harmonious cycle, as with the moon and the tides. We restore our body's homeostasis so that it can function optimally.

There is little to nothing for us to do. There is no need to push to enter the space of *yoga nidra*. We simply lie down, relax, set an intention, listen, and respond to the voice we hear telling us to put our attention on our breathing or scan through the body, placing attention on specific points in turn. As we go, we learn to communicate with our body using its preferred nonverbal language of sensations, emotions, images, and energy. This ancient approach is founded on timeless wisdom that has never been more vital than today.

Yoga nidra takes us beyond the limitations of the so-called rational mind—which is not rational at all! We see that mind for what it is—a mass of distortions—because it identifies with our memories of past experiences, especially traumas. We realize we are not our distorted thoughts and no longer identify with this thief that would rob us of our presence. In *yoga nidra*, we leave behind the thinking, driven, memory-laden paradigm that hides our being. We free ourselves from its habits, judgments, expectations, and stories.

One of the secrets to *yoga nidra* is how effortlessly it allows us to enter the world of the third eye (the sixth chakra), where the nonjudging witness consciousness is housed. One of its purposes is to open this energy center, which belongs to our physical body yet is not part of it.

Thought to be anchored to the physical body at a point located between the eyebrows and a few inches back into the skull, the third eye is part of the subtle bliss body (the *anandamaya kosha)* that is an unbounded awareness at the center of our being. This point is the link between our subconscious mind and the superconscious states of transcendent experience. Here we can awaken our nonlinear intelligence, including intuition and creativity.

There is a series of steps in the practice of *yoga nidra.* After setting our intention, we induce tension in the body, followed by relaxation. The tension in the first half of the sequence puts the body into contraction in order to release stagnant or blocked energy in the second half of the sequence, the relaxation phase. As energy is released and floods the third eye, the body's natural harmony is restored. The rational mind has gotten out of the way, so we can enter the domain of being. This is where healing at the deepest levels occurs. In deep relaxation, we are able to tap into the universal energy within and around us, aka the field or source (the language used to describe it varies). This energy is free and readily available to everyone.

Once we have shifted from duality to polarity, we experience ourselves as being in a state of unity with all else that is present. This offers us a foundation on which we can form authentic, resonant connections with others.

Yoga nidra produces a positive, calming effect on the nervous system, helping practitioners overcome insomnia, chronic pain, anxiety, depression, and more. It has also been demonstrated to offer a significant reduction in stimulation of cortical input to the deep brain, mediated in part by the dopamine system involved in our pleasure and reward structure.

The last thing leaders want is to reduce their cortical and executive functions! But our rational minds hijack us and impair our executive function on an ongoing basis, so it is important to learn how to temporarily pause and reboot our minds, so that we can enjoy being fully present during the remaining hours of our day. This allows us to experience inspired thought and action and connect with ourselves and others from an integrated perspective.

CHAPTER 6

Connect
Create Real Communication

I define connection as the energy that exists between people when they feel seen, heard, and valued; when they can give and receive without judgment; and when they derive sustenance and strength from the relationship.[1]

—BRENÉ BROWN

To connect is to open the gateway to who we *are* while closing the door on who we *are not*. To do so, we need to drop any preconceived ideas that reside within us. We need to release old habits of judgment and reactivity so we can enter conversations with a beginner's mind, listen with attention, and speak with respect. We need to drop in and become present and integrated before we can connect and be curious about who and what is in front of us. One key to being able to connect is feeling safe enough to do so—and the workplace is not always a safe place.

According to the American Management Association (AMA), a 2007 poll of 1,000 adults by the Employment Law Alliance (ELA) found that "44 percent of American workers have worked for a supervisor or employer who they consider abusive. Among the instances of abuse the ELA poll's respondents had witnessed or experienced at the hands of a supervisor or employer were sarcastic jokes (60 percent), public criticism of job performance (59 percent), 'interrupting . . . in a rude manner' (58 percent), yelling or raising one's voice (55 percent), and 'ignoring you/co-worker as if you/he/she was invisible' (54 percent)."[2]

And the news gets worse. "Some bosses go beyond bad and become bullies. These kinds of managers and supervisors are also in large supply, according to findings from the 2021 U.S. Workplace Bullying Survey conducted by Zogby International for the Workplace Bullying Institute (WBI), a nonprofit think tank. The survey was the largest of its kind, with 1,215 respondents."

According to the WBI/Zogby survey, one-third of U.S. workers— about 79.3 million people—have been bullied at work, and most of the targets—57 percent—are women. The percentage of people who witnessed bullying was 19 percent, bringing the total to 49 percent of Americans who either experienced or witnessed workplace bulling. The survey reports, "The vast majority of bullies are men (67 percent), with 58 percent male targets and 42 percent female targets. Thirty-three percent of all bullies are female, with 65 percent female targets and 35 percent male targets."[3]

The report states: "workplace bullying is many things. It is sub-lethal, non-physical violence at work. It is emotional abuse causing emotional injury. It is status-blind harassment, but unlike its discriminatory cousin, it is not yet illegal in the U.S. It jeopardizes its targets' psychological safety. And it compromises targets' health and well-being through the involuntary onset of a host of stress-related diseases that can kill." Workplace bullying is defined as "abusive conduct that is threatening, intimidating, humiliating, work sabotage, or verbal abuse."[4]

The lack of positive relationships at work is a significant contributor to workplace disengagement as well. A 2019 article in *Graziadio Business Review* states: "Gallup tells us that people who admit to having a best friend at work are less likely to leave than those who don't. [And] you want them to be engaged with their manager—15 of the top 20 drivers of an individual's engagement relate directly to his or her immediate supervisor."[5]

Not surprisingly, our poor relationships at work exact a high cost on our mental and physical health. Many researchers in recent years have studied the link between illness and management. Stanford University professor of organizational behavior Jeffrey Pfeffer, author of *Dying for a Paycheck,* and two academic colleagues published a stinging 2015 report in *Behavioral Science & Policy,* a leading peer-reviewed journal. Their paper estimates "120,000 extra deaths annually in the U.S. from harmful management practices, and that extra health-care costs were $190 billion each year. That would make the workplace the fifth leading cause of death, worse than kidney or Alzheimer's diseases."[6]

And this is not a solely American problem. The UK government agency Health and Safety Executive reported data showing that 17.9 million workdays were lost in the United Kingdom from work-related stress, depression, or anxiety in 2019–2020.[7]

In a 2019 article posted on his *Truly Human Leadership* blog, Bob Chapman, CEO of manufacturing company Barry-Wehmiller, cites a 2019 study on workplace productivity published in the *Journal of Occupational and Educational Medicine.*[8] Three significant findings from the study:

1. Individual employees lose the equivalent of 31 workdays per year due to health-related issues, both mental and physical—and some are associated with on-the-job injuries.

2. Poor mental and physical health accounts for more than 84 percent of lost productivity.

3. Ninety-three percent of the subjective factors that affect workers' job performance, like dissatisfaction with the work and lack of

support from supervisors, ultimately are expressed in symptoms of poor mental and physical health.[9]

"People are our most important asset." These words are often written in the mission statements that appear on websites and in annual reports. Yet what happens within organizational walls too frequently doesn't reflect these sentiments and is a demonstration neither of good connections nor even of goodwill.

Clearly there is a gap between organizations' good intentions and how these intentions are, in fact, being lived by people who are feeling disconnected and may be in over their heads. Although the research data shows how workplace relationships and effective communication have as much power to positively impact people's health as poor communication does to adversely affect it, leaders still need to know not only *what* to do, but *how* to do something that matters for their employees.

As a conscious leader, you need to learn to *connect* to improve wellness. And it is your responsibility to create the conditions that make your employees feel safe enough to connect. From connection comes communication, and excellent communication markedly improves results.

The workplace is one of the most fertile grounds in which to plant the seeds of growth and resilience in the people we lead. Many individuals are more receptive to consistent feedback on their behavior at work than they would be from family members at home. Our workplaces can become spaces in which we learn and practice new, more enlightened ways of engaging and interacting with colleagues that can strengthen and support them and us. Most of us will spend more time at work in our life spans than we do with our loved ones, often forming close relationships with our work colleagues.

There is a common perception in organizations that people work for external rewards like money and status. Not only does that diminish what genuinely motivates people to work, but it's also a way for a leader to abdicate responsibility for the impact they have on others. In his groundbreaking book on motivation, *Drive*, Daniel H. Pink shared research on what actually promotes employee engagement and motivation and developed a new model that focuses on *intrinsic motivation* as a source for innovation.

Intrinsic motivation consists of three things:[10]

1. *Autonomy:* the desire to direct our own lives
2. *Mastery:* the urge to make progress and get better at something that matters
3. *Purpose:* the yearning to do what we do in the service of something larger than ourselves

This model is conducive to the type of connected leadership we are envisioning here.

How to Create Real, Connected Communication

Conscious leaders do their own inner work so they can co-create with others to solve problems. The possibility for co-creation begins with the inner experience of connection.

Lack of self-connection is felt in the energy of our professional relationships. Does this story sound familiar? A client once told me that he had been "listening to a colleague talking to me, and the whole time he was talking, I was thinking about what I was going to say to him."

He added, "I hate it when I do that."

And I would bet the person speaking to him hated it, too. When people sense our impatience or inattention, they may feel pressured or dismissed, and they can tell the message isn't fully landing on us. It's as if they've launched a rocket into outer space and it's overshot the moon. If this happens repeatedly, they likely will begin resenting you and stop attempting to communicate. That's bad for business, especially if you need to sign off on decisions and other operational matters.

Remember, communication isn't just about one person talking and another listening. In order for us to have *real* communication, a bond of connection is required. My client was so consumed by his repetitive thoughts and future orientation that he was not present in the conversation with his colleague and no bonding occurred. Because he was not a relaxed communicator, he couldn't genuinely connect and later regretted the missed opportunity.

Connection relies on presence and relaxed communication. Both are necessary to create an environment of safety and trust in which collaboration and co-creativity can flourish.

Reactivity: The Number-One Impediment to Connection

Reactivity is a reliving of the past, or a "re-action." It shows up in our energy field and manifests as a pattern of shallow or held breath, muscular tension, hasty communication, and agitated vocal tone. When we are in a stressed, reactive mode, we cannot connect to others—we are disconnected from ourselves and not paying attention to details.

Time pressure is a massive source of stress for most people. To relieve it, we shift into high gear and are likely to skip the steps that help us connect. Impatience interferes with our creativity and destroys our peace of mind.

When we are in a reactive state, we are disintegrated. A common problem for high-performing businesspeople is being "violent" toward ourselves by ignoring or overriding our physical need for food, water, sleep, and human connection. In reaction, we are energizing the things that disconnect us.

Others are affected by encountering our stressed and reactive mind. If we express a judgment of them because we are reactive and critical, we may reinforce their self-judgments, in which case we are participating in amplifying their negative self-talk. Co-creativity is not possible then, as people become inefficient when they judge themselves.

Generous words, pay increases, or any other extrinsic motivating attempts will be ineffective for anyone whose energy field is distorted by reactivity.

Responses Are Truth, Reactions Are Lies

There are different levels of engagement the personnel in organizations experience. The first of these is complete disengagement, which is a big problem that *absolutely* must be addressed. Then there is cooperation, which is better, because it means people are at least going along with their leader's or co-workers' plans. Collaboration is *even* better. This is when teams of as few as two and possibly many more are working in tandem to help implement the organization's plans. Co-creation steps engagement up to the highest notch, where the creativity that is occurring is innovative— it's like bringing ideas straight out from the ether.

For people to engage with one another on any level and feel invested to any degree in accomplishing the aims of an organization, you need real communication. This is where mental and emotional reactivity can get in the way.

As we've established, reactivity is caused by past conditioning. Our "triggers" hurt us, and they hurt other people as well because they prevent connection. The thing about reactions, however, is that they are phantoms. If we *identify* with our reactions—in other words, if we believe they define our character or personality—we limit the range of our perceptions and abilities in the present.

Neither co-creativity nor collaboration can take place for us when we are frustrated, irritable, or judging others. If we react, we cannot truthfully engage with others in the present. All leaders, especially *emotionally triggered* leaders, need to do inner work to become less reactive because of how fast and far their reactivity can ripple through an organization. Wise leaders might even consider introducing methods to help reduce other people's stress and boost their inner connection and awareness.

A lack of connection is the biggest barrier to inspiring the creative potential dormant within each of us. The antidote is for us to relax, drop in, and integrate within ourselves before we communicate with others.

Fortunately, you now have the tools to do this! As we've been discussing all throughout this book, you can center yourself by breathing deeply and tuning into your energy by simply noticing the sensations in your body. Also be clear about your intention to integrate your being, become a witness and connect, and then deliberately open your heart. This last step will allow you to leave the domain of your thinking mind and ego dominance.

If we disidentify with our reactions and fears, we can stay present, and communication and co-creation can take place. The measure of connection and co-creation in our relationships reflects our internal state of harmony and wholeness—or *dis*harmony and fracture.

When we're fully engaged and co-creating, there is no need for conflict or force, so we never lead from anger. At this level of engagement, we drop any attachment to persuading and winning. We release any sense of needing to control or prove we are right or have all the answers. We take responsibility for our own way of being instead of expecting others to make us whole or give us what we want.

To foster a sense of safety and establish co-creative conditions, we ask questions such as "How can we make this work together?" We accept what other people have to offer, even if we don't agree. And because we are being receptive, open, and connected, we have access to our creative impulses and inspire others to access theirs as well. Trust and innovation can flourish.

Connection originates in the energy of love, from which we can access our higher intelligence and creativity. Love helps us resolve any internal conflicts before we interact and communicate with other people. Instead of looking to others to get what we want, we begin with ourselves and the understanding that how we are *being* is affecting them.

When we operate in this way, we are in the present. Connection unfolds naturally.

Loving Leaders Create Connection

To partner with others and recruit them to turn our visions into reality, we need to bring heartfelt emotional connection into the way we work with our teams. Organizations need leaders who are openhearted. Such leaders can communicate their vision, increase good energy, and open other people's hearts as well. Co-creative teams are marked by people who are connected to themselves, so they have the capacity to collaborate and connect with others.

When a leader encounters a person with a tendency for self-rejection, they can help this individual embrace their potential. Everyone is looking for acceptance, and a leader can offer a colleague unconditional acceptance, regardless of that person's prior beliefs or past experiences.

As leaders, we often have no trouble accepting others as they are even though we struggle with self-acceptance. Yet our acceptance of people must start with us. We cannot expect others to embrace self-acceptance if we do not practice it ourselves.

Creating Conscious, Compassionate Communication

Violent communication takes many forms. The most obvious ones are when we use threatening language or speak in an angry tone of voice. But what about the way our word choice conveys judgment or dismissal of others? Are we aware that sarcasm and criticism are also violent? Seemingly benign words can wreak havoc on others.

When we say *you are* to another person, what follows is often a label. For example, we might say, "You are weak, you are scattered, you are lost . . ." After hearing critical comments such as these, people will play the harsh words over and over in their minds, and it wounds them. If our comment triggers a traumatic memory and its associated feelings, the listener may believe it to define who they are—*identifying* with it. In this manner, the harmful words we use, as well as the way we say them, can destroy our ability to connect with listeners.[11]

Furthermore, if we speak harshly to someone, we may regret it and chastise ourselves mercilessly, which can also be traumatizing and triggering.

At the yogic level, the origins of violent communication rest within self-judgment. When we speak in harsh ways, we are disconnected from the love and harmony that is our true nature. Our language reflects our conflicted and possibly self-critical inner state of being.

Simply *trying* to use nonviolent words is inadequate. Even if we choose the "right" words, the lack of harmonious energy will be felt. Instead, we can aim for inner connection and a desire to reveal our true nature. When we live in a heartfelt, loving manner, the need to check violent impulses becomes superfluous.

The Vedic objective for communication is to speak in a kind and loving way, so that our words are synergistic with our compassion for ourselves and others. The root of all good communication requires that we first be in internal harmony—in other words, *we need to communicate with ourselves in compassionate language and describe ourselves respectfully because our ability to express ourselves to others evolves in parallel to the evolution of our inner state.*

When we restore our natural harmony, we are no longer hurting ourselves and can begin to heal. Then we can reach out to others and speak to them from the perspective and energy of harmony.

To reiterate: You cannot build harmonious communication on a foundation of inner discord. But what can you do about it? When you notice you're experiencing an internal conflict, become curious as to the cause, and then gently investigate what this problem or triggering event is provoking within you.

Consider these questions:

- What emotion am I experiencing? Name it.
- How does this situation resemble other times when I felt a similar emotion?
- What do I notice occurring in my body, my mood, my thoughts, my emotions? Feel the sensations as they arise.
- Am I angry at the person who triggered me, or am I thankful that they have pointed out my triggers (reactivity that is within my control)?

As leaders, we need to clarify what we care about and share our values with others. If co-workers on a project are using judgmental language to talk to or about one another or sound agitated when communicating, it is appropriate for you to step in and model connected communication—and to help them let go of their fear and manage their reactivity. Consider asking them these questions:

- What is happening here right now?
- What has happened on this project that is preventing you from moving forward?
- How is it similar to or different from other situations you've experienced?
- What can you do to resolve this issue?
- What's one step you agree to take to move forward?

Once people feel connected, they will open up, contribute in meaningful ways, and have the potential to interact in a co-creative manner.

LEADERSHIP IN ACTION
The Impact of Learning to Connect

Tony was the COO of a high-growth entrepreneurial company. When we began working together, he characterized the culture of his organization as "frenetic, reactionary, and moody." He aimed to "eliminate the bad habits that happen when people don't perform to my expectations. I can be volatile. When I get hooked on a perceived flaw or failing, I have a hard time containing my emotions. I want to improve my emotional agility and find a better way to communicate my frustrations."

Tony was already open to change, and he was ready to learn. His challenges had pushed him to the point where he was ready to let go and try something new. After listening to his struggle to connect successfully, I decided to teach him to drop in. Initially, I offered him the chance to have a direct experience of himself through dialing into the sensations in his body instead of pursuing his habitual thought patterns. I also had him practice dropping in at least once a day.

Tony noticed shortly thereafter that he was "no longer getting hooked by the anxiety of others." He also said, "I observed my pulse, jaw, and hands and did not get caught up in an escalating drama at the office. Instead, I got present and listened."

Over time and with practice between our coaching sessions, his responses deepened. "I see now that I had been reacting and not responding," he admitted. "The physical and mental practices you have taught me have helped me lean back and enter the moment. This takes me out of cognitive escalation. For me, mental and emotional reactivity happens when I am not being present, and I can see that I am giving up power and control when I get into that state.

"To be open when I'm talking to my executive team, I now know to center myself, to breathe, and to drop into my sensations. When I do, presence, stability, and patience are more achievable. I'm not taking in others' reactivity the way I used to. I'm joyful that I am breaking the old patterns of communication I had. This could be a whole new way of relating."

Several months into our coaching, Tony shared his excitement at having created a morning routine to help prevent himself from getting agitated before he hit the office: "Today, I dropped into a meditative state. I felt the energy field around my body. I was in a stable 'place,' a profound state of acceptance. My mind shut off. I find this inner quiet very exciting, and I'm enthusiastic about sharing it. Good things are happening in my relationships."

Another month or so later, he further reported, "I've been able to sustain new energy on an accelerated path. Acceptance is key. When someone cascades into me with dominant energy, I move my own psychic energy out of the way. Theirs doesn't derail me or push me off my island of tranquility. I've learned that when I have a reactionary response, it's an escalator, a magnifier, a multiplier. When I drop in, I can access the insights my colleagues need from me. It allows me to be more thoughtful in my responses to them. Detachment from expectation and my own awareness are the keys. As I relax and breathe intentionally, I can become a witness to myself and others. I can engage in a nonjudgmental way to inspire collaboration.

"At work today, we had a team session in which I observed two colleagues in conflict with one another. Throughout it, I was able to manage my natural triggers by focusing on my breath and dropping into my body. I'm very happy to report that when I feel anxious or agitated now, I can recalibrate a dozen times if necessary. I'm very grateful for that."

Tony was so tickled by his personal results that he hired me to work with the rest of the leaders in his division. After the program was well underway, he reported: "The work you've been doing with me and the team has substantially elevated our game. Everybody is celebrating here. Maybe it's simplistic to say, but acceptance and learning to absorb energy rather than just reflect it, really matters. I myself have learned to redirect my energy so that it comes from a base of acceptance, and it's helpful. People need to be seen, heard, and accepted, and I am able to give them this. Before our work together, my energy was the opposite of what my heart was trying to accomplish. I now see that my mind is crafty, and I don't want to 'eat' what it's 'serving'!"

He continued, "Susan, the progress you've made with us is jaw-dropping. Colleagues are really changing. I've really changed! Intimacy and trust are increasing among us. People are less guarded. I'm awestruck that we have been able to create a cohesive leadership team, considering how poorly we were interacting when we started. I would love to spread this mindful, compassionate conversational style throughout the organization."

Tony's example shows the power of a leader focusing on communication. He did the work for himself, and his relationships changed. He also reported that his level of personal satisfaction at home increased significantly as well.

Establishing Resonance: Leading by Deliberately Amplifying Energy

Consider the idea of *resonance* as it applies to sound. When two notes occur in phase with each other, they are amplified. For example, a fine lead crystal glass will vibrate at a particular frequency. If a singer emits and sustains a note at that same frequency (often helped with amplification), the vibrations of the glass persist and continue to increase in strength until the glass shatters. But if the singer were to sing a different note that did not match the crystal's frequency, the glass would not break. Likewise, active noise-canceling headphones work through a mechanism known as *destructive interference.* They create their own sound waves, which are similar to the incoming sounds, but 180 degrees out of phase, thereby canceling each other out.

All people naturally gravitate toward that which is pleasurable or *resonant* with their own energy and steer away from that which is painful or *dissonant.* When two people are energetically resonant, their being is amplified because their essences and intentions are in phase. Because they are "moving in the same direction," they can enter a state of co-creativity.

In a business setting, we seek to establish resonance through identifying common bonds. With emotionally intelligent people, this often happens organically. A technique we can practice to strengthen this capacity is to make a personal inquiry that shows curiosity. If you have a strong enough relationship with them not to be perceived as overstepping personal boundaries, you may express compassion. Ask about their day, their health, their family, their hobbies, or other overlapping interests. Blended with the perspective of the Eastern wisdom traditions, resonance takes on an additional meaning that incorporates attention and energy.

It's hard to listen to music when we hear dissonance between the notes. It's also hard when we're picking up static. Similarly, it's hard for us to hear a message when there is static in our head. For us to resonate with others in our role as leaders, we must not create static within us—a leader needs to emit *clear* energy. If our intentions are not clear, others cannot know with what they are resonating—or hoping to. Instead, they hear or feel our static.

Whether static or clear, however, we cannot control other people. They must vibrate freely, both at their own clear frequency and in phase with us, for communication to come from connection.

Once we are aware of our clear frequency and resonance, we can tune in to the frequency of others. And once we are resonant with their frequencies and resonances, everybody involved can tap into the shared field of amplified energy and gather what they need from it.

When I coach a group of co-workers, for example, I typically help the team calibrate their internal energy state at the outset of our calls or meetings. Next, I invite all participants to share a *check-in,* a one- or two-word description of what they are feeling.

We then set our intentions, discuss what we wish to have accomplished by the end of our time together, and energetically attune ourselves to one another to determine how we are going to work together for the duration of the conversation or meeting. We may choose to engage in joint breathing exercises to help the team relax and integrate.

As the leader of the call or meeting, all these steps help me focus on creating both cognitive and energetic resonance among team members. Attuning to "where" each person is in the moment allows us to find a frequency in ourselves that will help us match one another.

Dissonance Must Be Addressed Early

If you do not yet fully appreciate how important it is to take a few minutes to establish connection at the start of a meeting, consider the following example of destructive interference in an organization. I was working with the CEO and her team. The number-two person, the COO, was a man who was having a damaging impact every day on his colleagues and direct reports. He lacked the skills necessary for connection and brought so much dissonance into routine business meetings and interactions with direct reports that he was blocking co-creation at every turn.

Week after week, I had been hearing from everybody individually about the problems that were being generated by this executive's way of being with others, both one-on-one and in group settings. Prior to doing in-person work with the executive team, I had to clear my bias to ensure that I would not judge him. I wanted to be neutral and simply curious as to how he would behave when we were all together at last.

Early in the session, he began to test me, and when he discovered he could not enrage and provoke me to get the anxious response he normally evoked from others, he tried drawing in my cofacilitator to test the waters there.

When I debriefed with the CEO afterward, I said, "You know you have an 800-pound gorilla in this organization, so what are you going to do?"

She replied, "We've tried everything. He doesn't want to change; he wants to change everyone else. People are leaving—in fact, people have left. What I mean is, this guy is now costing the company money and talent. I have had more people within the organization tell me that if something isn't done very soon, they will also leave."

We reviewed the specific controlling behaviors that the second-in-command was using to get his way and showed how they were creating dysfunction throughout the system. I saw two options: one was to offer him the chance to do some serious work on his leadership behaviors and plan to change them. The other was that if he declined to work on himself, he would be asked to leave the organization or be relocated to a different role.

The CEO said, "I'm not saying that I'm not willing to try, but I'm not very hopeful that he's going to change. No one has ever taken him on. There have been people in my position before me, but none took him on. Other companies have dismissed him."

Following this conversation, I spoke with the senior human resources manager to discuss my plan, and she said, "You're more compassionate than I am."

I replied, "Perhaps. But I see a human being who's trapped and doesn't know another way to be. If he knew another way, he would be working differently, in a manner that would provide him with more ease and flow in his world and in which he could do more of what he cares about. But he doesn't know how. What I perceive is that he is unable to accept himself and has a habit of rejecting others before they reject him."

I had evidence that he was impulsive and self-absorbed. When I was in a meeting with his co-workers to which he wasn't invited, he interrupted us twice by knocking on the door and seeking attention. The CEO informed him, "We've paid Susan to come in and work with us. This isn't the time."

He brushed her objection aside, saying, "This is important. This needs to be done in five minutes."

He interrupted again later in the day. After our group meeting had ended, as I was saying goodbye to the CEO, he entered her office and said, "I hope you didn't think that I was being disruptive."

She replied, "As a matter of fact, you *were* being disruptive."

From this exchange, I concluded that he likely had a sense that what he was doing was disruptive and offensive, and yet he kept repeating it. Previously, other consultants had been brought in to assess his behavior through a 360-degree review process so he could learn the impact he had on others. He apparently had attacked the consultant who delivered the results, dismissing the final review and firing the news bearer.

My ultimate analysis was that although the COO had numerous strengths that were of benefit to the organization, his behaviors were unacceptable. Chiefly, he was unable to connect with others, defensive, and not receptive to individual behavioral work with any coach, so he was unlikely to improve. Given this report, the CEO chose to remove him from a role in which others reported to him, giving him a new position in which his behavior would not have an impact on direct reports or equal colleagues for the time being. This gave all parties a chance to assess what could be done to leverage his strengths constructively, while preventing continued damage to the system from his negative behaviors.

As a leader, if you can identify the frequencies at which each person resonates, you can conduct team meetings in a harmonious manner that leads to productive communication, shared ingenuity, and a robust and integrated outcome. You may wish to ask yourself questions before a meeting, like: Why does someone not fit into our group? Are we aligned? And if not, what can I do to help increase resonance? When hiring, consider: Is this person resonant with our team and our company culture?

Leaders who are willing to try can learn to recognize thought patterns in themselves and others that lead to resistance and dissonance. Begin by examining your thought patterns, habits, and other things that stir up resistance—reviewing the types of events that you have recently found triggering is a good place to start even if it's a bit uncomfortable for you. Remember, you must create harmony within yourself to harmonize with others.

For leaders to resonate with others, we need to let go of preconceived beliefs, judgments, and ingrained habits. We need to be able to recognize our reactive triggers and have compassion for ourselves when they emerge.

An example of thinking that holds us back is: "Big risks are dangerous. It's always better to take the path of least resistance."

Contrast that with: "I trust that I will know when I am on the right path and be able to clearly see the next steps I need to take, no matter the risk, when I am connected within."

An essential skill for co-creative communication is dropping in, which we explored in Chapter 4. To drop in, we notice our internal landscape. We check in on our personal resonance and communicate from this energy because we know that connection is only possible when we focus on our *own* way of being.

By this point, you've acquired most of the skills you need to connect one-on-one or in groups. Keep practicing the techniques you've learned and challenge yourself to use them whenever you get the chance. Test them out in phone calls, internet chats, and face-to-face conversations. As you integrate them, you'll discover what resonance feels like and see its positive effects, and you'll increasingly trust your ability to connect and how far it can take you.

If dissonance destroys creativity, how does resonance promote it? If 100 musicians are playing by themselves, all you have are 100 notes. However, if those musicians come together to form an orchestra, they can create a harmonious sound that is greater than the sum of their individual instruments. In jazz, not only do the notes harmonize, but they also serve as co-creative stimuli for the other notes.

When we work co-creatively, we can move from disconnected options to inspired solutions. When we are in resonance, we can realize unexpected possibilities.

Elements of Team Building from a Vedic Perspective

A thorough review of effective team building is beyond the scope of this book, but here is a basic list of the top seven elements that apply to leading all sorts of teams:

1. Create a relaxed atmosphere prior to having team conversations.
2. Identify people who do not resonate with the team, and work on establishing harmony before expecting collaboration.
3. Build trust incrementally with others so the foundation of safety is never compromised.
4. Find a way to connect with each member of your team, and create opportunities for them to connect individually and bond with one another.
5. Create a sense of shared purpose.
6. Assign tasks and duties that build on your team members' previous successes and strengths.
7. Describe your successes in the context of the team, focusing particularly on team connection, trust, and collaboration, not just on productivity.

Connection Within a Team Enables Co-Creation

Connected leadership permits people to be joyful as they accomplish their goals. When all the individuals on a team are going through the sequence of steps required for effective self-connection before they set out to establish a team connection, the team responds as a living entity to this resonance. It develops a sense of shared purpose in fulfilling its mission that usually feels very rewarding, even if their tasks are difficult or tedious.

Just as we each contain complementary opposing forces within us, a team possesses these qualities, and a team that can harness and balance its polar forces effectively will develop a strong foundation for co-creativity and well-being. Such a team has the potential to become a highly focused, remarkably self-sufficient entity over time—and one requiring little oversight. The human connections within the team are fundamental to establishing trust, collaboration, and breakthrough results.

LEADERSHIP IN ACTION
The Connection Map for Leaders

Tess was a company founder and CEO whose business depended on her ability to connect. But when we met, she was experiencing difficulty in getting others to connect to her vision for the company. She told me, "What gets in my way is not feeling able to prioritize sufficient time to make [the] connections that have been offered. What has really stopped me, the issue underlying my reluctance to connect, is my fear of not having the perfect answer or of not appearing to be expert enough when I do follow through."

In Tess's case, stress was also a pitfall. Under stress, people don't usually reveal their true self, and she wasn't centered enough to show her true self to her staff and customers. She reported that she "couldn't think clearly" when she was geared up and needed to get more conscious and connected and move her breathing down to her gut. "That's a better place for me to operate from," she said. I was pleased to hear she was so self-aware.

As Tess practiced opening, learning, letting go, and integrating on a daily basis, she began feeling more relaxed and centered, and she was able to bring more of her natural being into every interaction. But when she deliberately followed the steps of the Connection Map for Leaders (see the list below) during meetings and conversations, the transformation in her energy was palpable. People would ask her, "What just happened?" They were intrigued, and then she could draw them deeper into her vision of what was possible for the company. When she was in alignment internally and "operating from her gut," she found she could face the world with authenticity.

In her words: "When I'm connected within myself, the energy flow is clearer, and conversations and partnerships come together more easily."

Follow these steps when you want to initiate co-creation:

1. Let go

2. Drop in

3. Integrate

4. Resonate

5. Connect

6. Co-create

Tess also tried following the Connection Map for Leaders in a meeting with a high-stakes prospect. She prepared by focusing on clearing the static in her energy. She also phoned me, and we discussed her mood and the emotions she was experiencing in anticipation of the conversation. She worked to let go of reactive elements in her thinking that were triggers for her.

Tess also acknowledged the importance of being fully present with the individual in front of her and not prejudging them either before or during the conversation. When the meeting began, she allowed herself to simply be curious about the prospect. To do so, she had to let go of any fears or worries about the extent of her own knowledge, the prospect's likes or dislikes, and her desire to convince them that her approach was the right choice. She just allowed her new style of communication to unfold.

By staying focused on what resonated within her that she felt was relevant to her prospective customer, while remaining detached from the outcome, she could reflect on the conversation without losing her way. Shifting her attention from her goal to the needs of the person she was talking to helped her forge a connection on the basis of their shared values. As a result, she landed a new, very lucrative contract.

Tess was impressed that her newfound ability to be present allowed her to listen deeply and create a level of engagement that produced immediate results. Often, it's not about how much we know but how we are being—and connecting—that counts. Learning to trust—both yourself and the process—is an important part of the leadership journey.

Ayurveda: A Leadership Hack for Meeting People "Where They Are"

As a coach, I have learned the importance of meeting each individual where they are. Coaches don't use the same techniques with everyone because we know that individuals process information in many different ways.

As a business leader, co-creating with your team will also take different forms, depending on the individuals involved. "Where they are" matters. But how do you find their "where"?

In the West, we tend to focus solely on cognitive or personality differences in people, but we have seen throughout this book that embodied and energetic issues are foundational for connecting. Ayurveda, the sister branch of yoga that encompasses lifestyle and nutrition practices, is a shorthand way to assess what needs to be addressed within teams energetically to optimize them.

Our constitutions, or natural inclinations for how we engage with the world, impact our abilities. Each person is like a symphony made of different sections, such as woodwinds, strings, brass, and percussion. Although we each contain all these sections, our bodies' energetic systems emphasize them to different degrees. The way in which we maintain homeostasis differs based on our constitutions, and thus the lifestyle and dietary choices that keep us functioning optimally—food, sleep, and other elements of self-care—vary as well.

Organizational leaders should strive for all sorts of diversity on their teams, not just technical or functional abilities. Certainly, we ought to explore how individuals have varying tendencies to access and digest information. Organizations often conduct assessments of individual personalities, leadership abilities, and cognitive and behavioral styles to seek out this diversity. Yet these assessments cannot even begin to account for the nuances of our unique constitutional differences, nor do they help people adjust their diet and lifestyle to optimize their well-being, using knowledge of the three *doshas* (see "20 Complementary Qualities of Experience to Balance" on page 118).

Just as people with two different energy profiles access the world differently, they can co-create completely different answers to any specific issue yet achieve similar outcomes. Consider Aesop's fable about the Tortoise and the Hare. We initially think that the speedy yet overconfident Hare will win the race, but then we learn that the slow and steady disposition of the Tortoise works more effectively. Although both animals were capable of making forward progress, their natural inclinations and dispositions give them differing abilities and advantages.

For example, Ayurveda teaches us that people with:

- *Pitta* (fire and water) constitutions are likely leaders, entrepreneurs, and CEOs or other roles where assertiveness, ambition, and risk-taking are needed.
- *Vata* (air and space) constitutions often display high levels of creativity and vision. They excel in roles that rely on communication and creativity and offer flexibility.

■ *Kapha* (earth and water) constitutions often excel in roles where they are healers, supporters, and caregivers—or anywhere else that strength and stability are required.

Just as any team benefits from including members with varying experience levels, problem-solving and team-building capabilities, genders, ethnic/racial/cultural backgrounds, and perspectives, it would also benefit from incorporating individuals with different *doshas*. As a leader, knowing the Ayurvedic constitutions of team members could also help you respond to their needs when they're under pressure and out of balance. Ensuring that the teams we build contain an array of constitutions can be helpful, as this will contribute to a diverse array of solutions to any situation.

CHAPTER 7

Illuminate

Become an Inner Switch Leader

We but mirror the world. All the tendencies present in the outer world are to be found in the world of our body. If we could change ourselves, the tendencies in the world would also change.[1]

—MAHATMA GANDHI

Throughout history, the contrast between darkness and light has been prominently featured in art and literature as a symbolic struggle between evil and good in the human character. In the modern era, this duality has also been showcased in cinema, in everything from Hollywood westerns (black hats and white hats) to *The*

Lord of the Rings and *Star Wars* film series. We are drawn to these narratives because, intuitively, we understand that the struggle between darkness and light will persist in humankind and in us personally for eternity—and that it can never be fully resolved. This conflict is one reason people gravitate toward religion and spirituality.

On the physical level, we know that daylight comes when the planet rotates toward the sun and nightfall when it rotates away. We also know that when we walk into a dark room and flip a light switch on, the darkness recedes—albeit temporarily. We feel confident that when we switch off the light, the room will become dark again.

From our observations of natural and electric light, we Westerners have concluded that darkness represents the absence of light—within us as well as in the sky. But from an Eastern, Vedic perspective, which emerged in written form from the region that is now India more than 3,000 years ago, the resting state is viewed as light, not darkness. And on an individual level, the reason for doing practices like yoga is not to turn on a light that will penetrate and illuminate our inner darkness, but to *remove* the darkness that is preventing us from perceiving our natural inner light. That darkness is understood to be obscuring our light, lying over it like a blanket or filter—or to be polluting the ember of divine light that shines naturally through our being. Like the moon can eclipse the sun, the light of our being can be blocked from our sight.

Can you see how significant this difference is? Both physically and metaphorically, from the Vedic perspective, we are beings of light, connected to one infinite source of light, which merely becomes hidden or muddied or eclipsed.

In the Vedic terms that are inherent to yoga, love is an energy of light, while fear is an energy of darkness. Many practices from the Eastern world are designed to help us remove our own darkness—to liberate ourselves from it. Then our natural tendency to embody light can spontaneously express itself without effort. The focus of these practices is always on removing any darkness that resides within us—any fearful beliefs, false identities, and self-limiting habits. Once those are eliminated, our love, peace, bliss, connection, and creativity can shine.

We know from physics that light is energy and that everything in the cosmos, tangible or intangible, arises from within a unified quantum field of energy, including us and the five *koshas* that are dimensions of our being (see Chapter 4). The bliss body, as we've discussed, is the subtlest and most radiant dimension of who we are that we can consciously access. What is important to know is that we *really are light*. The darkness is what's inauthentic.

Light possesses the capacity to catalyze self-organization and growth, while darkness catalyzes decay and dissolution. Any removal of darkness—of who we are *not*—allows for a fuller manifestation of light and love that helps us reclaim, reveal, and express our true light.

Our collective task as leaders is to shift the paradigm in our workplaces and in broader society to become *removers of darkness* for ourselves and for others.

What Is a Remover of Darkness in a Leadership Context?

Contrary to popular belief, the word *guru* does not translate to a sage, mystic, leader, or priest. In Sanskrit, it means "remover of darkness." A guru has learned to live immersed in a state of loving energy. They have made the inner switch by lifting up the veil of darkness in their mind, heart, and body through good knowledge and good practice. They can now spontaneously express the light of the infinite presence within them.

How is becoming a remover of darkness relevant to becoming an effective leader? Leaders' true power comes from removing their own darkness and revealing their inner light. When they do, they can use their presence to connect with the people they lead and help them remove their own darkness and reveal their own inner light. Thus, leaders who make the inner switch are removers of darkness, illuminating the way wherever they go.

In every scenario, it is urgent that we learn to ask ourselves, "Who or what is leading me right now? Is it my loving presence? Is it my ego?" Much of the time, we appear to be led by our thoughts, feelings, and emotions, and, as we have seen, these are often reactive and self-protective. The ego mind creates both reactions and expectations, which are based on hurtful memories of past events and fears of what might happen in the future. These dark energies play on the screens of our minds and trick us into believing they represent who we are. Our fears then create walls around us that keep us immersed in darkness. When we defend the walls, we are defending our fears and reactions.

It's as if who I am *not* sees what is *not now!*

The ego mind often leads us to find solutions born of our internal conflicts, and we then create more conflict around us. For example, our discomfort in a particular situation might lead us to behave in ways others perceive as aggressive or unhappy. That could trigger someone else's insecurities, and they respond with their own defensive or aggressive postures. Now we have created or exacerbated the very conditions and relationship dynamics we originally feared. This is how the ego brings the energy of darkness into our lives and the workplace, making it harder to see the light.

Many of us have big dreams that we never fulfill. Although we want to have and be whatever we want, our inner power is diminished by our fears. We live in proverbial darkness, constricted by walls of insecurity. While growing up, we absorb the idea that the world is not safe. Undigested emotions from traumatic events haunt our present-day lives, so we create emotional walls to protect us from further pain. (It merits pointing out that this wall-building is done unconsciously.)

Before co-creativity can occur in any organization under our leadership, we must take down the walls that hide our inner radiance, release our inborn capacity for clarity and connection, and show our colleagues and employees a path to reveal and express their own light. They, too, carry within them this birthright of freedom and light. Everybody does.

A leader who has made the inner switch possesses the ability to evoke a conscious co-creative response in others. To be an Inner Switch Leader means to accept and honor the fact that the response we wish to see from another *always* begins within us. To lead and collaborate effectively, we cannot demand, control, or manipulate others into doing what we wish—that only creates more fear, self-doubt, resentment, reactivity, and darkness to pollute the workplace. The engine of our actions needs to be the power of our inner light and openheartedness.

One important caveat: Even though an Inner Switch Leader comes from a position of open, connected energy, remember that it is neither necessary nor appropriate in an organizational setting to express love physically to anyone. Maintaining healthy boundaries is responsible and ethical. You also don't have to love (or even like) people in your heart—such emotions shouldn't be faked or forced. What is necessary is that you demonstrate compassion, empathy, respect, acceptance, inclusion, and connection to everyone.

Leaders possess a singular power to activate and inspire the creative spirit within others. To do this, Inner Switch Leaders need to prepare themselves to create and hold space for others by following the path laid out in previous chapters. To illuminate any situation—i.e., to be a remover of darkness—drop in, integrate, and connect. Release attachments, judgments, and preferences. Witness what *is* in the moment. Do your best to disidentify with conditioned fears from the past and abandon habits that arose from painful past experiences. Align with the energy of connection, as this is the ultimate source of co-creativity.

Darkness in itself is not a negative thing—it is part of the balanced polarity we aim to embody. Consider the polarity of day and night. The dark of night is neither *for* nor *against* the light of day. The energy of the sun can be used to make food, bring life to the earth, and provide warmth. But it also has the potential to burn and obliterate humankind and destroy the world. So, too, with darkness. The energy of the moon impacts the tides and migration and reproductive patterns in some animals. We sleep and rejuvenate our bodies and minds in the nighttime.

When darkness occurs within a balanced polarity, it can be natural and beneficial. If the darkness we experience, however, is internal darkness that is self-imposed through mental and emotional conditioning—such as recycled criticisms about our abilities and value as people—we eclipse our true self with its shadow. Dwelling in dark emotions can be a sign that something is amiss.

Darkness that obscures the true light of our being is what Inner Switch Leaders seek to remove, first in themselves and then, by stimulation and inspiration, in others.

How Does Healthy Polarity Apply to Leaders?

As we have previously discussed, in Chapter 2, leaders tend to maintain our bodies in a state of duality through the constant overdrive of our sympathetic nervous system (SNS). In this state, we use various methods to blow off steam, some healthy and some unhealthy. These include everything from exercising, shopping, and gambling to the consumption of alcohol, drugs, and food. Overreliance can result in addiction.

We have also established the importance of living in polarity within the dynamic range of homeostasis to keep our bodies functioning optimally. Our bodies are naturally designed to live within the range of action and reaction at an unconscious, autonomic level. Our biochemistry ebbs and flows along with diurnal rhythms, so that we alternate between activity and dormancy. Living in a state of balance allows us to exploit the inbuilt mechanisms of our physiology to purposefully relax whenever we find ourselves in a stressful situation. In fact, homeostasis is the only state in which we *can* drop in and integrate. It is also the state in which we can most effectively digest food and process trauma.

Stress can be fully "digested" as it occurs so that it does not linger in our emotions and body to become or evoke a conditioned response. In homeostasis, stress simply passes through us, causing only *temporary* discomfort as it is processed. This is why I am such an advocate for yoga: It offers us a complete structure within which to promote and restore homeostasis. Through direct experience, it teaches us that the universal intelligence that animates life can be experienced within the sensations of our individual bodies.

On the yoga mat, we begin with integrative intention and then consciously put our bodies into a posture that *creates* tension. When we let go of the tension, we see that we don't have to *do* anything to relax; relaxation happens naturally.

When we attune ourselves to our sensations through observation, we tap into universal energy and intelligence. As we awaken our energy through regular practice, we can function at higher levels than were previously possible for us.

While we are doing business, we can also use a stressful situation like we would use a challenging yoga posture if we invoke an integrative intention at the outset. For instance, when we are entering a tense meeting or about to engage in a difficult conversation, we can pause to become centered, present, integrated, and connected.

We also benefit from setting aside a few minutes after the meeting or call to relax, breathe, and allow homeostasis to occur before moving on to our next activity. We can use the yoga mat to train ourselves to stay in natural homeostasis so that we can eventually apply the same approach in other areas of our lives.

There will be times when we are subjected to trauma. Traumatic situations cause tension in our bodies and arouse intense emotions. If we suppress our feelings or move on too quickly because we wish to avoid dealing with our emotions, we deprive the body of engaging in its naturally occurring homeostatic processes to regulate itself. Any avoidance prevents us from fully processing the trauma. When we ignore or suppress our feelings, we often store the trauma within our bodies, where it can cause all sorts of physical symptoms, many of which don't fully manifest until years later.

Although we can't always avoid or prevent bad things from happening, if we allow ourselves to feel pain and process our thoughts and feelings as it occurs (or soon thereafter), the pain recedes spontaneously, as with any other discomfort. It is only when we move on too quickly without naming and experiencing our challenging emotions that the pain of them becomes stuck within us. Once pain takes up residence, it colors our perceptions and reduces our ability to withstand the pressure of subsequent challenges, as well as interferes with our capacity to experience joy.

Previously suppressed pain can be triggered by anything that resembles any part of the moment in which the trauma was embedded. A smell. A sight. A sound. Even the way someone looks or speaks or situational dynamics can bring it all back with shocking immediacy. We carry so much inside us that if we don't learn how to continually process and release it, our behavior may be colored now and in the future.

When visiting Kathmandu, Nepal, during an early stage of our spiritual growth, my husband and I had the good fortune to meet with a very senior lama. We left the meeting with far more wisdom than we had possessed before. However, we must have also left more scrambled energy within the room than was there when we entered. As we were descending the stairs, we heard a sound emanating from the room—the lama's Tibetan bells. He was using harmonic resonance to re-center from the stress we had brought into his presence.

In retrospect, the placement of those bells next to his chair demonstrated his understanding of the use of integrative intention to relax after exposure to stress. He knew how to digest the impact of scrambled energy in seconds so he would be ready for the next visitor. The bell served like a palate cleanser, an intermezzo between courses at a dinner party.

As Inner Switch Leaders, when we take advantage of moments to restore homeostasis in our lives and let our intention for integration guide us, conflicts tend to dissolve on their own. This is a sign that we have broken free from the chains of the ego mind and entered nonlinear reality, an energetic field of higher awareness and presence. Here, we can access the subconscious mind and have intuitive breakthroughs.

An Inner Switch Leader Is Like a Self-Cleaning Oven

Although good knowledge is the foundation for good practice, the removal of darkness is not accomplished only by learning more information. It is actually a process of *unlearning* our attachment to our memories and our mental and emotional conditioning. Conditioning leads to expectations, but placing expectations on others harms us as well as them.

Here's an example of how the damage is done. If we focus on the times when others have disappointed us and carry those memories forward, we will be holding others hostage within the walls of our fears and distorted thinking. We become the judge and jury in every encounter in which we are not present in the now. If you're reactive like this, you won't illuminate what is right in front of you. Rather than expanding, you, your relationships, and your organization will contract.

When our attention is focused on our self-image or the ego mind's fears and anxieties, we cannot help others form connections to their own creativity. Our expectations will only reinforce their preconceived self-judgments, worsening their outcomes.

There is no way for another person to break free from our self-imposed restrictions when *we* are unable to do so ourselves. Any action we take from a conditioned state of expectation and fear will produce conflict.

Inner Switch Leaders learn to become the human equivalent of a self-cleaning oven. They have learned how to release unconscious habits and conditioning so that they are no longer held hostage by them. Such leaders do not create external conflict because they understand how to maintain pure, positive energy internally, no matter what issues they face.

An Inner Switch Leader is poised to enter into a collaborative process with others in which innovation and breakthroughs become the norm. They model "response-able" (responsible) leadership—choosing a thoughtful response based on what is present now.

Inner Switch Leaders Aim for Success Without Stress

Although leaders can achieve success without debilitating stress, many of us were not taught this way of leadership in business school or the workplace. We have instead been encouraged to be efficient, to multitask, and to drive ourselves and others to excel, no matter the consequences. Our bodies, therefore, come to house a tremendous amount of emotional residue.

If we lead by valuing efficiency at the expense of energy, it is almost inevitable that we will damage our relationships and health. If we have internal conflict as we work, we may be able to temporarily suppress this emotional energy, but it will come out elsewhere.

Energy is the vehicle of communication that can shift us from reactivity to responsiveness. An Inner Switch Leader aligns thinking and doing with feeling and being, facilitating homeostasis. Setting an intention while in an integrative state enables them to shape action into being—moving unmanifested ideas and plans into manifested physical form.

Inner Switch Leaders are fully integrated within mind, body, and heart. They tap into their inner harmony to access the stable, dependable leader within. This allows them to be intuitive, wise, innovative, inspiring, and successful without succumbing to stress.

One area of business that is of critical importance to leaders is how they make decisions. In my work as a coach, I see how challenging it is for many of my clients to gain clarity about the decisions they need to make. How do they ensure that a decision is not based on fear but instead comes from an open, expanded, and even loving perspective?

Decisions made out of fear degrade an entity. Fear when doing business leads to breakdowns in the relationships within and around the organization, and ultimately to its destruction.

By contrast, decisions made in the spirit of love and connection allow for spontaneous organization of people and ideas. Higher intelligence becomes accessible, and flowing creativity becomes possible.

I invite you to engage with the phenomenon of connecting to your higher intelligence experientially rather than cognitively. Aim to drop in through the relaxation of your SNS using one of the techniques we've previously explored (with the exception of *kapalabhati pranayama,* the breath of fire that accomplishes "skull illumination," which is meant to energize the SNS). Once you feel inwardly connected, you can immediately sense whether a decision is coming from love (meaning that you can trust it) or from fear or ego defense (meaning you may wish to revisit it).

How Will You Know When You Are Embodying Your True Self?

Because energy follows attention, when you are reactive, all your energy is deployed to address whatever has your hackles up or makes you anxious. When you find yourself reacting rather than responding, how do you stop and access your true self—the one that has been hijacked?

In a reactive state, you become enslaved to your mind's intense reactions. Your first step, therefore, is to notice the reactivity. The next is to regroup by using the Inner Switch leadership practices. Once you are reoriented, you can focus your witnessing intention on your tension, frustration, anger, or other emotions and experience them as energy. Just by witnessing blocked energy—being neither for nor against it—you can metabolize it and let it flow through you. When our egoic self disappears, our presence is revealed. Viewed with the nonjudging intelligence of the third eye, energy blockages can convert into prana and be integrated into a healthy system.

This is the point where we can touch the energetic presence that we are and experience our connection to the universal energy that is always within us. It is available at all times, though we do not always see it or feel it due to our own emotional coverage—experiences from the past that have imprinted in our minds—that hides it from our perception.

This is where our roles of attention and energy reverse. Instead of energy following attention, as it does when we are reacting, now our attention follows our energy. This is the exciting moment when we become an Inner Switch Leader. Energy is the wellspring from which we can attune to the flow of who we truly are. From this fountainhead, all our actions self-generate from polarity—every level of our being balancing naturally in the present moment.

Witnessing presence is where spontaneous creativity, co-creation, discernment, and free choice all originate. It is the only domain where it is possible to transcend who we are not.

In other words, just as we can use our breath to consciously access the autonomic nervous system, we can use a similar practice to access our subtle energy systems. As we witness the stored energy blocks created by undigested fears or anxieties from an integrated, embodied way of being, we metabolize the stuck energy and convert it to nourish the presence that we are.

Inner Switch Leaders Step Back so Others Can Step Forward

Once integrated into our presence, Inner Switch Leaders inspire others to tap into their own infinite source of power and creativity. Our ability to inspire others depends on the quality of our communication, and this in turn depends on the degree to which we feel harmonious within ourselves. Remember, Inner Switch Leaders use energy and emotions—not dominance—to connect with their colleagues and teams.

Consider my senior-level client John, who needed to conduct a conversation with an associate in his organization. His objective was twofold. He intended to:

1. Learn more about the associate's goals and aspirations for advancement to partner
2. Offer constructive feedback around an important behavioral change required for such advancement

In the past, John had held numerous conversations with the associate about a type of behavior that was distressing to colleagues. With remote work, the behavior became less frequent, and the complaints diminished. I let John know that the associate's behavior might be helping him satisfy an unmet need. We discussed that in order for him to change, he would need awareness as well as the desire to come up with a replacement behavior that would meet the same need while making a positive impact on his work relationships. John could support him in devising this solution.

To help John prepare to enter the conversation with the associate in "coach mode," I invited him to practice asking open-ended questions from a place of curiosity and spaciousness with me. That helped him identify and let go of conditioned thoughts and feelings about the process of coaching and his relationship with the associate. His intent was to remain open, relaxed, and neutral when they met. This was very balancing and grounding for him.

John decided that next he would share the positive qualities that everyone admired about the associate while acknowledging his potential for advancement within the firm. He would then check in with the associate by asking, "Where do you see yourself going within the organization? What are your aspirations?"

The key to establishing a connection and open dialogue here would be the quality and nature of John's listening to the associate's response. Whenever we hear someone speak, although we understand the words, their remarks are filtered through our conditioning. This is different from true listening, a heartfelt perceptual experience in which there are no filters. With true listening, we bring a full, openhearted presence and energy to our witnessing of the other person's thoughts and ideas. We drop our preconceived judgments and expectations for a certain outcome and stop planning what we are going to say next.

In heartfelt listening, we can hear what is said as well as unsaid. The other person feels heard.

Finally, John would ask, "Do you see any obstacles for yourself to attaining these goals?" In the best-case scenario, the associate would hopefully mention the behavioral concern that had previously been addressed. At this point, John could invite him to suggest a small step he was willing to take to change this behavior from one that was distressing to his colleagues to one that was conducive to their trust. The conversation would conclude with John asking, "What do you need from me/us to assist you in being successful with this change?"

In a conversation such as this, both parties are connected, exchanging what they care about, learning more about each other, and making and receiving commitments that elevate both the individuals and the organization of which they are a part.

A few days later, John entered the conversation for real with harmony and intention, and co-creativity resulted. The associate was engaged so that instead of floundering, he established the necessary conditions to subsequently flourish at the organization.

Leadership is a form of tutorship. Inner Switch Leaders create an environment in which other people can succeed and lead from integration rather than conflict. An Inner Switch Leader teaches others the technique of tapping into the master key that will unlock the dormant power hidden within them—energy management.

The only thing a leader can control is their own energy. Then through modeling and mentoring, they can inspire others to do the same.

It's important for a leader to be an open, accepting presence for others. This does not mean that they don't have expectations or set goals. It doesn't mean they are pushovers and doormats. It does mean they clear their past judgments when they engage with others and invite people to co-create goals and make commitments.

As co-creative leaders, we can inquire along the way: How is it going? What is working? What obstacles are you encountering? What are your possible options? What did you choose to do? How can I support you in your work process?

In such a line of inquiry, when done in the right mood, people come up with their own answers, and they will be motivated to act on what they themselves discover and commit to doing. For this to occur, the leader must hold a bigger vision for them—often bigger than the one the individual has for themselves.

An Inner Switch Leader offers the safe space of unconditional acceptance so that others can embrace that acceptance of themselves as they are right now. As a worker's self-confidence and self-image expand, it will impact their home life and personal relationships as well. Becoming an Inner Switch Leader is a privilege, as it potentially enables you to uplift many people.

Of course, John's conversation with the associate could have taken a wrong turn. The associate could have resented his questions and become hostile or been unwilling to modify his behavior. But an Inner Switch Leader takes the lead no matter how other people behave.

In the martial art of aikido, we move away from an attack so that its energy will pass us by. Similarly, if we don't enroll in another person's energy at the office, it cannot derail us. We must fall prey to our own reactive anger to become entangled in a conflict.

LEADERSHIP IN ACTION
How His Personal Transformation Enabled Kevin to Make a Companywide Impact

Kevin is a founder on the Inner Switch leadership journey, but neither of us knew it at the time we were introduced. Through the arc of our work together, he became an early catalyst for my seeing the Inner Switch leadership process systemically. When we first began working together one-on-one, the situation at Kevin's work was requiring him to change. Like many hard-charging entrepreneurs, he had done most of the jobs in the company at one point or another. As his company's head count grew, he had little tolerance for others whose work and accountability ethics or communication styles didn't mirror his own. It was clear to Kevin that he had a leadership problem but not how to handle it.

At the outset, Kevin described his challenges: "I'd like to see myself as a better, more integrated leader. I want to be able to engage people at the conversational level beyond fear and reaction." He realized that he needed more awareness of the impact his words and actions had on his team and became intrigued with the prospect of developing his emotional intelligence.

His initial coaching goals were hefty. He said, "I want to become aware of how I communicate to others, including my body language; to understand the people and situations that trigger me to become reactive; and to learn how to clear my mind proactively so I can remain calm and confident, instead of going into either a fight-or-flight mode."

Back then, Kevin was in the first stage of his Inner Switch leadership journey, and the challenges he was facing were causing him to question many of his long-held beliefs and assumptions. But he was willing to change and do the hard work of self-inventory, self-reflection, and self-modulation that is necessary to evolve as a leader.

Remember, the second stage of the journey is learning. In our initial sessions, Kevin was curious about all that he didn't know. I suggested articles, books, and audio files to him, which he devoured willingly. After working with me for a couple of months, he reported: "I am learning to achieve self-awareness and self-control; to have an honest, compassionate awareness of others; and to guide my staff without being directive and practice this as my leadership style." He was applying the same insatiable curiosity to the process of recognizing and overcoming his blind spots as he had to successfully filling a market need as an entrepreneur.

The third stage in becoming an Inner Switch Leader is letting go. This is actually an ongoing process, skill, and personal choice as much as it is a stage. Kevin was open to the possibility of letting go of his certainty about his perspective on himself and other people. I introduced him to somatic exercises that helped him center himself and foundational practices to create calm and inner strength. He committed to doing these regularly and diligently whenever he felt the need. In the process, he became more familiar with his internal state of being and how to regulate it. He observed his conditioned responses and released the blocked energy that was keeping them stuck in his body.

The fourth stage, which overlaps with letting go, is dropping in. As Kevin began to center himself regularly, he noticed things beginning to shift in his awareness. He stated, "Compassion begins with us. Who I am is my connection with love. The love I embody affects others. I can substitute compassion and love for judgmentalism. The first step is awareness. When I find compassion within myself, anxiety does not show through. I've discovered that the more I practice, the more letting go just happens without my doing anything consciously to bring it about."

Kevin was in the initial stages of learning to let go and drop into his natural lightness of being when he said: "I'm learning that practices do create good states. I'm most effective when I'm in a good place to begin [with]. Letting my thoughts come and go. That's sort of the point, isn't it? Now I practice my centering and breath work in the mornings at home and then take a moment before meetings so I can better control myself. As I learn to manage my inner state, my moods and emotions allow me to have more compassion and curiosity for others. I've had two people this week tell me they see the difference in me already. They said that lately, I seem light and more enjoyable to be around. I'm learning that what serves me in my role is to slow down, be open, control my reactions, and be in the moment. When I do, I'm confident and comfortable."

As you know by now, dropping in is also about dropping in to the present moment. I admired Kevin for investing so much of his heart in his journey of personal transformation and making such powerful progress. *One of the great benefits of liberating ourselves from darkness is that our mind, body, and spirit appear lighter and brighter, and it is as if we are coming home to ourselves. We may even like ourselves more.*

Four months from when we began coaching and including his commitment to personal practice, Kevin entered the fifth stage of the journey, the stage of integration. He noticed how all the previous stages were beginning to make a palpable difference, both within him and in the people around him. Smiling, he told me, "This process is so good. You can't tell the mind to do something by changing only your physical mindset. The real learning is that thoughts can come and go, and then choosing to let them go! I have been incorporating breath work into my practice. As I center, I'm feeling less anxious. I have reached a new level of 'me-ness.' I'm less reactive and domineering."

The sixth stage involves developing connections. Kevin had always thought he would earn respect through directive leadership and demonstrating a strong personality. This was an ego-driven approach to leadership. When he became aware of the importance of connection, he could see how this had generated admiration from some people, but not necessarily respect.

In one of our coaching sessions, Kevin reported on a new discovery: "Respect is listening. People want to be heard and recognized. Because of my intent to create connection, I have a new focus. My relationship with my direct reports is changing because I'm listening. Now I understand their hopes, dreams, and desires well, if not perfectly. Things are going better because of the nuance and sophistication of asking good questions."

He continued, "These days, I start by approaching everyone with compassion. I've been complimented on this by many people this week. In fact, I can see how much I'm being observed—and always was being observed, though I didn't perceive it before. People are noticing the changes in me. Creating space for connection is not dependent on my mood. It's a choice."

The seventh stage of becoming an Inner Switch Leader is illumination. Kevin said, "I've had a eureka moment. In doing this work, I now have the tools to see how physical awareness leads to new mental awareness. That is magical! In my training with you, I've received integrated tools to recognize when 'not good' is my own fabrication; when the voice of worry [and] judgment can exacerbate that. It's very hard work to be present. I'm doing daily breath work, and it's really, really working. I take five breaths, and with each inhale and exhale, I focus on one of these five elements: self-control, compassion, curiosity, communication, or confidence.

"My efforts at managing my own energy are working. I'm doing meditative breath work three times daily. It really helps to bring me to a calm state of presence. I use it to reset my approach if I'm going into a meeting. My top goal is to be a compassionate listener and then not react. I try to keep my point of view out of the way. We've begun to use centering in our meetings. I want to make use of it at work, as it is of great value."

He continued, "Your practice with me has elevated me into my CEO role in a new way. I see reactions differently. One of the biggest blockages I see is constant reactivity everywhere. It's a state of being. It descends from having answers vs. having questions. The distinctions I learned in the exercises you've given me have been very helpful in learning the distinctions in mind and body for myself.

"I'm moving from reaction and judgment to compassion, wonder, and communication. I'm working hard to walk and talk with a proactive and compassionate voice. I'm delighted with others' energy. I see it now, whereas I didn't see it before. I'm learning what love and compassion really are—an amplification of the need for self-awareness and control."

And he concluded, "We were never trained as listeners. We are celebrated more for being actors—for our bravado—than we are for making space, showing compassion, or illuminating others. My personal goal is to turn *compassion* into an action verb."

Kevin shared that at the time of our work together, shareholders were celebrating that earnings were up and on track for meeting ambitious goals for the year. The mood at the company was celebratory. There was a great deal of positive energy showing up in teamwork and collaboration. He stated: "Harmony is huge for me—I want more harmony and communication. It's going well, and things are falling into place. We're producing good results. Harmony is more evident every day.

"Now when we have meetings, we co-create as to how to have them. We center ourselves before beginning. How to create collective and individual growth? We choose one topic and set an intention for what we want to have at the end. We begin meetings with a check-in and intention setting—we let everyone say what they need from one another today. We celebrate what we have accomplished in the week preceding.

"We see ourselves as sensitive, compassionate leaders. We actively recognize the needs when one of us is off-center. We pay attention to that. We acknowledge that when one of us is hurting or out of sorts, we want to stop what we are doing and recalibrate. We are learning how to speak our piece and not get pointed at one another. We pay attention to keeping our energy aligned. When we are out of sorts, it spills into the rest of the company."

Kevin shared, "I'm committed to celebrating what I observe around me; I've learned that when you give people authority and share your vision, they'll amaze you with their ability to achieve the goals! We want to continue to hire good people, keep them, and treat them the way we want to be treated. We've come a long way with developing the language of our commitments, and this is expanding throughout the company."

As we were wrapping up our work together, Kevin told me, "The company is at last in the fine-tuning stage." Soon thereafter, Kevin and his company reached their goals and enjoyed a significant liquidity event.

In summary, what Kevin learned from our work together was:

- Increased self-awareness
- Self-control
- Honest, compassionate awareness of others
- How to guide and lead without being directive

He practiced this style of leadership through:

- Exercise
- Meditation
- Delegation
- Sharing
- Acknowledging
- Enjoying

I was amazed at Kevin's experience and saw its potential to influence others. After reading Kevin's story, I hope you are feeling inspired and enthusiastic about everything that is possible for you and your organization through your work to remove the darkness eclipsing your true light. Does it feel like the sun is coming out?

Key Principles for Becoming an Inner Switch Leader

By this point, you should understand that Inner Switch Leaders use daily practices designed to help them disengage mentally, emotionally, and physically from their work and the outer world. They know they must awaken the Inner Switch Leader within themselves to remove their own darkness and facilitate this for others.

The Inner Switch Leader is the light of consciousness who sees what is in the present for what it is. The more separated we are from the source within us, the more conflict and separation we create with everyone with whom we interact.

Key principles to remember as you continue this journey are to:

- Open your heart and incorporate its wisdom in your decision making. The brain seeks to codify, organize, label, and interpret what the heart experiences. But how you feel matters just as much. Consider your heart a vital component of leadership.

- Take the lead *no matter how* any other person behaves. Shift away from your reactive perceptions of how someone is being or has been. It's important to notice if you are becoming "edgy" in your communication so that you can disengage from any reactions in your mental, physical, and emotional bodies. And please remember that you can interrupt unwanted thoughts and feelings using the technique of slow breathing with long exhalations. The point is to consciously self-regulate by activating your parasympathetic nervous system (PSNS).

- Embrace that it is your responsibility and role to affect the energy field around you. By doing so, others can access the light of their Inner Switch Leader—it will be as if a line of candles is being lit, beginning, but not ending, with you. You are shifting from being a conflict creator to an integrator of everything the moment brings—even difficulties—including diverse opinions, agendas, and people.

- *Always* choose openhearted connection and joy instead of fear, suffering, and domination over the people you lead. The path we walk in our daily work will become the outcome we see, and you are more likely to get the outcome you desire if you are joyful along the way.

- Begin the day with an integrative intention. Create harmony within yourself before extending your energy and engaging in external communication with others.

- Center yourself before meetings—and continue centering during them if necessary. Use proper, slow, belly-breathing techniques with long exhalations to soothe your SNS. Feel your bodily sensations shifting as relaxation sets in.

- Create spaciousness in your speech patterns to allow for the full expression of your thoughts and feelings and to give people openings to respond.

- Focus on becoming a more present observer. Your aim is to see things as they are now instead of reacting to your stored memories of the past.

Guidelines for Illuminating Conversations

When you're speaking with someone, aim to:

- Visualize the other person and truly see them for all their positive qualities.
- Connect with the person as they are right before you. Look at them through direct eye contact and regulate your breath so that you see them as they are.
- Listen wholeheartedly, paying attention to the mood, emotions, and energy of the encounter. Look for signs of resistance or withdrawal in others.
- Encourage the person you're speaking with to reconnect with their true self.
- Harmonize with the person and inspire co-creativity by choosing words that are positive, empowering, and outcome-related.
- Respond to what is said from the perspective of an observer rather than a judge.
- Trust that the action that spontaneously follows inspiration is the right one.
- Align with the flow of co-creation and move forward with joy!

Love May Be the Highest Aspiration of the Inner Switch Leader

As leaders, we can use our business activities as a medium to cultivate our consciousness. We need to go beyond the notion of meditation as simply a method to encourage relaxation. It *is* that, but it is also essential for developing our ability to withdraw from reactivity in situations we find threatening. Dropping in allows us to remain connected and loving so that we can enter into co-creation. Meditation can help us withdraw and remove the darkness that prevents our light from shining as brightly as it can, for the benefit of ourselves and those we lead and love.

As we understand more about the role of energy in how we establish connection and the kind of conscious communication that leads to co-creation, we will naturally seek to embody more compassionate, kind, and loving energy. This is what we ultimately desire most of all.

The truth is that we are each responsible for removing our own darkness. Nobody can do it for us, and we cannot do it for another person. But when we are deeply connected to the energy of self-acceptance, we will naturally transmit this to others. Our presence will invite them to heal by finding a similar wellspring of belief in themselves and help them dive into their creativity.

Everyone is looking for connection, empathy, acceptance, and recognition. Unfortunately, many people do not accept themselves, based on past experiences that predispose them to interact as rejected and fearful beings. When a leader can initiate engagement with a wounded person from a place of connection—with an open heart—everything shifts. Love is an energy that can blast through barriers. All the potential that is locked away in their personal prisons of fear and self-rejection can be transformed into realization when we use our love to gently break down their walls.

The solution to the world's ailments is to create loving, connected leaders. Love is the highest aspiration of which we are capable because, as the Vedic sages, mystics, and enlightened yogis have said for millennia, love is the pure consciousness that is everywhere, around us, in us, and working through us. An Inner Switch Leader understands how to access this universal intelligence, which is far more powerful than our cognitive intelligence. Happily, the body offers us the certainty of a compass when we listen to our pure sensations of the moment and attune to their language. Decisions made with this awareness are always trustworthy, while those made with only cognitive awareness may not be.

An Inner Switch Leader knows how to access love within themselves and hold space for others so that they can remove their own darkness and experience the power of love and pure consciousness, too. When we are present, we can inspire others to do the same so that the solutions to attain our goals spontaneously appear. Moreover, this unleashed, energetic co-creativity improves the likelihood of a successful outcome, while ensuring a joyous journey all along the way.

Afterword

Although we have reached the end of this book, I hope its completion will mark a new beginning for you as a leader. Hopefully it has strengthened your desire and ability to continue learning and approach it as a lifelong journey that never ends. I invite you to use the book as a vessel to hold the elements of your personal learning journey as a leader. As you explore new things, you may see where they fit into a larger, clearer framework rooted in timeless wisdom.

Yoga offers a validated, comprehensive, integrated system for life and well-being. There is no first or last or highest or lowest limb of yoga. All eight limbs work together to support our return to wholeness. At times, you may be drawn more to one element of yoga than another, an attraction that will likely change over time. No matter where you begin, your knowledge, intention, and intuition can guide you from disintegration toward unity.

Life offers us a continuous set of postures and edges that we can use to notice how we are being in any given moment. When someone pushes one of your buttons, for example, you could interpret this as a gift offered to you and accept it as a lesson. You now have enough tools to approach any learning edge in life and leadership from multiple angles and to digest experiences at a reasonable pace, even if you cannot initially process them. Trust that as you release your discomfort around these experiences—and your identification with them—you are integrating them into a fuller expression of your timeless state of being.

Developing new habits isn't easy. Start with small steps in the direction of your intention, and don't be afraid to experiment. When you fall off the wagon, simply pick yourself up and get back on. Always be generous with yourself and grant yourself an unlimited amount of compassion along the way. As humans, we all deserve compassion. We must show it to ourselves before we can offer it to others.

Spiritual awareness comes and goes. Trying to retain an enlightened state of being is a fool's errand. The most spiritually attuned beings I've met told me they cannot hold on to their highest energetic level at all times. Even the Dalai Lama meditates for two hours before going out to meet the world and then continues his meditation and prayers for three hours after a walk and breakfast. As busy leaders, it's unlikely that any of us can set aside five hours a day for practice, so let's make space for enlightenment without grasping at it. When we set our intention on removing our darkness, the time we need to practice *will* spontaneously appear.

This book is a professional and personal roadmap to transform our way of being and create lasting legacies of connection, value, and care for one another. When we do, our organizations will reflect our better selves. This is the world I envision for all of us who lead.

It is my privilege to share this knowledge with you. In return, I'm asking you to use it to transform yourself, your company, and the world. Business leaders and organizations are uniquely positioned to transform our society. Although there are no regulations about displaying loving-kindness in the course of doing business, leaders can and should unleash it in their employees, customers, vendors, industries, communities, and other stakeholders.

Please take your knowledge, spirit, wisdom, and strength and use them to make a far-reaching impact on your business and your community. In the process, you will spontaneously improve the relationships in your personal life as well. We have the power and possibility to transform ourselves and the world we create in the present. What better legacy is there?

Finally, living with heartfelt love for yourself and all those around you will bring you absolute joy *all along the way.* When you realize you are experiencing this, it is a sign that you, too, have become an Inner Switch Leader.

Designing a Regular Practice

To improve and eventually maintain our abilities, we need to develop daily practices and lifestyle habits. There is no single right way to do this because each practice needs to meet a different individual's needs. But the first step in every case is having an intention to practice at all.

A while back, I had a yoga teacher who told me, "When you find yourself in tough times, you don't *ascend* to the level of your capability, you *descend* to the level of your practice." Those are words to live by. Practice affords us:

- A space to explore and try on new ways of being in our bodies
- A quiet time for reflection to increase self-awareness and create intentionality
- Fertile soil for creating new neural pathways. As psychologist Donald Hebb's assembly theory has been summarized: "Neurons that fire together, wire together."

We've had decades to create our current habits, but new, improved habits are merely a few months away with regular practice. It's important to remember that there is no such thing as perfection, only learning, discovery, and taking small action steps. Aim for frequency, not duration at first. Repetition is the friend of new neural habits.

There are many ways to practice. Some people like to do the same things every day, while others like to mix it up. Try a variety of ways until you settle on a system that feels right for now. You can always adjust as you go. That's why we call it practice! Aim for 10 to 20 minutes daily to start and work your way up from there. Your practices should be done on an empty stomach and include at a minimum some centering breath work, movement, energy work, and meditation.

You now have a basic framework for understanding the importance of dropping in as a way to become present. You also have a menu of options and techniques. What follows are resources with which you can experiment. There is no one-size-fits-all solution. I personally use different practices on different days, depending on what I need most. In time, as you develop confidence in your abilities, you will, too. Trust yourself and the process that is unfolding. Simply begin with a small baby step, done with care and frequency, and in time you will notice big changes have taken place. It will make all the difference in your leadership effectiveness.

Resources

Author's Website

Susan S. Freeman: SusanSFreeman.com

Resources for *Yoga Nidra*

Yoga nidra offers a complete system of deep relaxation. It is said that one hour of *yoga nidra* is the equivalent of four hours of sleep, as the body goes through all the stages of sleep. The following suggestions will help you get started:

- The Mindful Movement website has multiple resources on *yoga nidra*: themindfulmovement.com/?s=yoga+nidra

- Steve Wolf, Awase Publishing:
  awasepublishing.com/product-relax-cd.php
- Liam Gillen: youtube.com/watch?v=LSIN_MjsSTI

Additional recommendations are:

- I AM Yoga Nidra app, created by Kamini Desai:
  kaminidesai.com/transformational-sleep-app
- I AM Yoga Nidra immersion self-study course, offered by Kamini
  Desai: kaminidesai.com/yoga-nidra
- Amrit Yoga Institute: bit.ly/3lKWKfz

Resources for Ayurveda

Recommended books on the ancient art and science of Ayurveda include:

Ayurveda: A Life of Balance: The Complete Guide to Ayurvedic Nutrition & Body Types with Recipes by Maya Tiwari (Healing Arts Press, 1994).

Eat • Taste • Heal: An Ayurvedic Cookbook for Modern Living by Thomas Yarema, MD, Daniel Rhoda, DAS, and Chef Johnny Brannigan (Five Elements Press, 2006).

The Everyday Ayurveda Cookbook: A Seasonal Guide to Eating and Living Well by Kate O'Donnell (Shambhala Publications, 2015).

Unfolding Happiness by Ambika Devi, MA, and Vijay Jain, MD (Mythologem Press, 2016).

For high-quality Ayurvedic herbs and body-care products, I use Banyan Botanicals: banyanbotanicals.com/.

Resources for Clearing the Chakras

I sometimes enjoy playing wordless music in the background when meditating, such as a collection of tracks designed to harmonize the seven chakras: *Caroline Myss' Chakra Meditation Music,* composed and performed by Stevin McNamara (Sounds True, 2001).

Hypnotherapist and altered states therapist Cory Cochiolo leads a 33-minute-long guided meditation that I often recommend, "Best Chakra Clearing Practice Ever!" It is available on the Insight Timer app (for both iOS and Android) and website: bit.ly/3Iz1tcZ.

Endnotes

Dedication Quote

[1] Pema Chödrön. *The Places That Scare You: A Guide to Fearlessness in Difficult Times* (Boulder, CO: Shambhala Publications, 2018).

Introduction

[1] Carl Jung. Source currently unknown.

Chapter 1: Open

[1] Jeroen Kraaijenbrink. "What Does VUCA Really Mean?" *Forbes* (December 19, 2018), bit.ly/3IyJtQ0.

[2] Megan Reitz and Michael Chaskalson. "How to Bring Mindfulness to Your Company's Leadership," *Harvard Business Review* (December 1, 2016).

Chapter 2: Learn

[1] Rosabeth Moss Kanter. bit.ly/3Z3LAkv.

[2] Patricia Pulliam Phillips. *ASTD Handbook of Measuring and Evaluating Training* (Alexandria, VA: American Society for Training & Development, 2010).

[3] Caroline Myss. *Anatomy of the Spirit: The Seven Stages of Power and Healing* (New York: Harmony Books, 1996), pp. 96–101.

[4] Jon Kabat-Zinn. Taken from the title of his 1994 book on mindfulness meditation, *Wherever You Go, There You Are* (New York: Hachette, 1994).

[5] Will Durant, *The Story of Philosophy: The Lives and Opinions of the World's Greatest Philosophers*, p. 87.

Chapter 3: Let Go

[1] Stephen Mitchell. *The Second Book of the Tao* (New York: The Penguin Press, 2009), p. 97.

[2] Bessel van der Kolk. Taken from the title of the 2014 book on effect of traumatic stress on the body, *The Body Keeps the Score: Brain, Mind, and Body in the Healing of Trauma* (New York: Penguin, 2015).

[3] Linda Johnsen. "The Koshas: 5 Layers of Being," *Yoga International*, bit.ly/3IcybiZ.

[4] Michael A. Singer. *The Untethered Soul: The Journey Beyond Yourself* (Oakland, CA: New Harbinger Publications/Noetic Books, 2007), p. 94.

[5] The eight limbs of yoga are *yama* (restraint), *niyama* (observance), *asana* (posture), *pranayama* (breath), *pratyahara* (withdrawal), *dharana* (fixation), *dhyana* (meditation), and *samadhi* (contemplation): Stuart Ray Sarbacker and Kevin Kimple. *The Eight Limbs of Yoga: A Handbook for Living Yoga Philosophy* (New York: North Point Press, 2015).

6 Brad Walker. "Understanding the Stretch Reflex (or Myotatic Reflex),"
StretchCoach (May 13, 2019), bit.ly/3KAf71h.

Chapter 4: Drop In

1 "U.S. Employee Engagement Slump Continues," Gallup (April 25, 2022),
bit.ly/3XI7c4T.

2 APA Working Group Report on Stress and Health Disparities. "Stress
and Health Disparities: Contexts, Mechanisms, and Interventions
Among Racial/Ethnic Minority and Low Socioeconomic Status Popu-
lations," American Psychological Association (2017), bit.ly/3XFiDu6.

3 Ambika Wauters. *The Book of Chakras: Discover the Hidden Forces Within You* (Hauppauge, NY: Barron's Educational Series, 2002), p. 6.

4 Caroline Myss. *Anatomy of the Spirit: The Seven Stages of Power and
Healing* (New York: Harmony Books, 1996).

5 B.K.S. Iyengar. *Light on Yoga: The Bible of Modern Yoga, revised edition*
(New York: Schocken Books, 1979), pp. 44–5.

Chapter 5: Integrate

1 William Blake. *The Marriage of Heaven and Hell* (1790), bit.ly/3KhVlqQ.

2 "Integrate," Merriam-Webster.com (accessed April 22, 2021).

3 "What Is Newton's Third Law?" Khan Academy, bit.ly/3Z0qXFD
(accessed April 22, 2021).

4 Roy F. Baumeister, Kathleen D. Vohs, and Dianne M. Tice. "The Strength
Model of Self-Control," *Current Directions in Psychological Science,* vol.
16, no. 6 (December 2007), pp. 351–5.

Chapter 6: Connect

1 Brené Brown. *The Gifts of Imperfection: Let Go of Who You Think You're
Supposed to Be and Embrace Who You Are* (Center City, MN: Hazelden
Publishing, 2010), p. 19.

2 "The High Cost of Bad Bosses," American Management Association
(January 24, 2019), bit.ly/3IzPyvO.

[3] Gary Namie. "2021 WBI U.S. Workplace Bullying Survey," Workplace Bullying Institute (2021), bit.ly/3Kj0ZJj, p. 11.

[4] Ibid.

[5] Mark Allen. "The Real Costs of Bad Management—And What You Can Do About It," *Graziadio Business Review,* vol. 22, no. 1 (2019), bit.ly/3SbSQIw.

[6] Joel Goh, Jeffrey Pfeffer, and Stefanos A. Zenios. "Workplace Stressors & Health Outcomes: Health Policy for the Workplace," *Behavioral Science & Policy,* vol. 1, no. 1 (2015), pp. 43–52.

[7] "Working Days Lost in Great Britain," Health and Safety Executive (United Kingdom) (accessed September 13, 2022), bit.ly/3I9zY8A.

[8] Bob Chapman. "The Slow Burn of Poor Leadership," Truly Human Leadership (June 13, 2019), bit.ly/3Ei8xID.

[9] Ibid.

[10] Daniel H. Pink. *Drive: The Surprising Truth About What Motivates Us* (New York: Riverhead Books, 2009), Chapters 4, 5, and 6.

[11] Marshall B. Rosenberg. *Nonviolent Communication: A Language of Life, 3rd edition* (Encinitas, CA: PuddleDancer Press, 2015).

Chapter 7: Illuminate

[1] 1964, *The Collected Works of Mahatma Gandhi, Volume XII, April 1913 to December 1914,* Chapter: General Knowledge About Health XXXII: Accidents Snake-Bite (From Gujarati, *Indian Opinion,* 9–8–1913), Start Page 156, Quote Page 158, The Publications Division, Ministry of Information and Broadcasting, Government of India (Collected Works of Mahatma Gandhi at gandhiheritageportal.org).

Acknowledgments

My journey to a published book has been lengthy and involved many supportive people and enterprises. I am grateful beyond what words can express to the following:

My husband, Tom, for his steady and relentless commitment as a collaborator on this project. His interest in yoga brought a deep understanding of these principles. As an accomplished physician and neuroscientist, his contribution to the book was to bring linear, sequential thinking to concepts that Westerners often find difficult to grasp. His love and support of me in every possible way made this book happen.

The entire team at Entrepreneur Press, beginning with Hallie Warshaw, whose enthusiasm and endorsement of my material drew me to Entrepreneur; Sean Strain, for being a dream publishing partner, working with me in every aspect of the project in a collaborative, co-creative manner; Sheri ArbitalJacoby, fact checker; Wyn Hilty, copy editor; Karen Billipp/Eliot House Productions, production and composition; Andrew Welyczko, cover design. They are an author's dream team.

My agent, Leticia Gomez, of Savvy Literary Services, who brought me to Entrepreneur Press and has been the consummate partner, having exceeded my expectations at every stage.

My editor and "book sherpa," Stephanie Gunning, who believed in my vision from our first conversation. Her extraordinary literary talent and experience helped bring the book into the world.

The top-notch professionals whose wise counsel has guided me: Becky Robinson and the team at Weaving Influence; Lisa Berkowitz and Maureen Kelly for initial strategic marketing and public relations; Al Baiocchi of FrontPage Interactive, web designer; Tracy Kennard of Your Virtual Footprint, virtual and social media assistance since I opened my business.

My friends and colleagues whose hearts and minds guided me throughout the process, including: Rania Anderson, who introduced me to her book editor and got the process rolling; Maria Arnone and Stephen Stumpf, PhD, without whom I would not have become an executive coach, and whose early reads of the manuscript encouraged me; Dr. Marketa Wills, whose manuscript read led her to introduce me to my agent; Karen Sherman and Marlene Chism, friends, colleagues, and fellow published authors who generously shared resources with me.

All the many teachers and writers of yoga and Vedic philosophy who have preceded me. I stand on their shoulders, benefiting from the wisdom of the millennia that has been passed on as written and oral tradition. Their contributions gave me the foundation to embrace this learning as my own so that I could transform it into the novel system shown in this book.

Dr. Vijay Jain, whose love and dedication to Ayurveda added dimensions to my understanding of how the breadth of yoga offers wisdom for all aspects of living.

The leaders who have been my clients. Their receptivity to merging ancient wisdom with modern executive coaching techniques has helped me to refine and validate this novel approach to transforming Western leadership.

About the Author

Susan S. Freeman, MBA, PCC, NCC, is an executive coach, team coach, author, speaker and leadership development consultant. Her approach to Western leadership transformation integrates Eastern wisdom derived from more than 25 years of studying yoga and yogic philosophy. Susan is dedicated to helping leaders expand their influence and change the world by making the "inner switch." Through her novel "Inner Switch™" method, leaders lean how to shift from simply "acting" in the world to first "being" within themselves so they can influence others. Leaders experience improved relationships, health, and overall work and life satisfaction.

Her clients value her skill in helping them unlock the secret to true leadership effectiveness, connect strategy to execution, and increase trust, collaboration, and team effectiveness within their organizations. Susan brings to her coaching more than 30 years of corporate, entrepreneurial, and nonprofit business leadership experience. She is sought after by investor-owned companies desiring to reach the next level of growth and profitability. Areas of special interest include team coaching, challenges of entrepreneurship, powerful communication, cultivation of executive presence, and career resilience.

Susan received an M.B.A. with a focus on marketing from Columbia University Graduate School of Business and a B.A. degree in psychology from Wellesley College. In addition to *Inner Switch: 7 Timeless Principles to Transform Modern Leadership,* she is the author of *Step Up Now: 21 Powerful Principles for People Who Influence Others.* She is an accredited Professional Certified Coach with the International Coaching Federation, the largest coaching body in the world. She holds additional Practitioner certifications in Team Coaching from the Global Team Coaching Institute in the U.K. and in Coach Master Toolkit Consulting from the Center for Executive Coaching. She has been featured as a corporate speaker, keynote and on both television and radio. As a leadership columnist, she has contributed to *Entrepreneur* magazine, *Thrive Global, Elephant Journal, Authority Magazine, Valiant CEO,* and other national platforms.

Susan is also dedicated to the cause of empowering women. She serves senior executive female leaders as a core guide at Chief. She volunteers in a mentoring program at her alma mater, has served Davis College and the Akilah Women's Center, Rwanda in numerous capacities, including on the women's leadership committee of the Global Leadership Council. Passionate about education, Susan served as founding Chairman of an educational board at the secondary level, and on an advisory board at the university level.

Susan lives with her husband in the mountains near Asheville, North Carolina, and in Tampa, Florida. They have three grown children. She is an avid ballroom dancer, world traveler and hiker who is occasionally visited by the poetry muse.

Rarely a day goes by when she doesn't reach for a piece of dark chocolate.

Index

A

abusive bosses, 126–127

addiction, 48

agni (fire), 116

air and space (vata dosha), 116, 117, 118, 119, 145

air or wind (vayu), 116

akasha (space or ether), 116

alternate nostril breathing (nadi shodhana pranayama), 90–91

anandamaya kosha (bliss sheath), 80, 83, 84, 93, 124, 149

annamaya kosha (physical sheath), 80–81

apas (water), 116

asanas (postures), 40

autonomic nervous system (ANS), xxi–xxii, 88, 103–104

avoidance strategies, 48

awareness, 56, 58, 63, 76–77, 96, 103. *See also* koshas

awareness exercise, 19–20

Ayurvedic body-mind connection, 35–36

Ayurvedic concepts, 115–120. *See also* yoga
Ayurvedic resources, 176

B
beginner's mind (shoshin), 17–18
being present. *See* presence
being vs. doing, 7, 9, 27–29
being-based leadership hallmarks, 30–43
   about, 30
   consciousness and presence, 32–33
   energy awareness, 33–35
   mind-body connection, 35–38
   self inquiry, 30–32
   witness consciousness, 38–43
biases, 33
bliss sheath (anandamaya kosha), 80, 83, 84, 93, 124, 149
body, awareness of, 76–77
Body Keeps the Score, The (Van der Kolk), 52
body-mind connection, 35–38, 76–77
Book of Chakras, The (Wauters), 84–85
breath, 88–90, 109
breathing practices (pranayama), 90–92, 156
brow (or third eye) chakra, 87, 98, 112, 115, 123–124, 156
bullying at work, 126–127

C
Cartesian philosophy, 8
case studies
   connection (CEO and COO), 138–140
   connection (Tess), 142–144
   connection (Tony), 134–137
   dropping in (Amanda), 77–78
   dropping in (Sandra), 94–95
   illumination (John), 157–159
   illumination (Kevin), 160–165
   integration (Sandra), 107–109
   learning (Marianne), 39–41
   letting go (Keith), 60–62, 69
   letting go (Trisha), 50–51
   opening (Alan), 3–4
   opening (Theresa), 5–6
   opening (Vince), 17
centering yourself. *See* dropping in
chakras (energy centers), 34, 81, 84–88, 98, 103, 112, 123–124, 176
close-mindedness, 12–14
cocreation, 129–132, 141–142, 144–145, 150
cocreative communication, 16
collaboration, 130, 131
communication. *See* connection
complex regional pain syndrome (CRPS), xxi
connection, 125–146
   about, 125–126
   case study (CEO and COO), 138–140
   case study (Tess), 142–144
   case study (Tony), 134–137
   cocreation with, 129–132, 141–142, 144–145
   communication as essential to, 128, 129
   compassionate vs. violent communication, 133
   disconnected leaders, 9
   dissonance, addressing, 138–141

engagement levels, 130–132
loving leaders creating, 132
reactivity impeding, 130
relying on presence, 129
resonance, establishing, 137–141
team building, 141–142
conscious intentions, 110–111
consciousness and presence
hallmark, 32–33
controlling leaders, 1–3
cooperation, 130
criticism, 133
crown chakra, 87

D

darkness, removers of (gurus), 149
darkness and light, 147–151
decision fatigue, 114
decision making, 155–156, 165, 168
designing a regular practice, 173–174
disconnection, 130
disengagement at work, 127, 130
disruptive behavior, 138–140
dissonance, 138–141
distractions, 48
doing vs. being, 7, 9, 27–29
doing-oriented leaders, 30–31
doshas (energies), 116–119, 145–146
Drive (Pink), 128–129
dropping in, 71–99
about, 93
awareness, five layers of, 80–84
benefits of, 93–94
best time to practice, 96
body awareness and, 76–77
breath and, 88–92
case study (Amanda), 77–78
case study (Sandra), 94–95

chakras and, 81, 84–88, 98
defined, 72
dropping into presence, 71–76
integrated homeostasis in, 79
leadership presence, xxxvi–xxxvii,
71–75
learning how to become present,
75–76
letting go and, 96
mindfulness vs., 96
responding vs. reacting, 77–79
state of nondoing in, 79–80
dropping in exercise, 97–99
duality, 25–27, 46, 121–122
dug-in leaders, 1–3

E

earth (prithvi), 116
earth and water (kapha dosha), 116,
117, 118, 119, 146
edges, 55–56, 58–59, 65, 67–68, 114,
170. *See also* letting go
eight limbs of yoga, 58, 170, 178n5.
See also yoga
emotional intelligence, 8
emotional reactivity, 77–78
employee engagement and
motivation, 128–129
energies (doshas), 116–119, 145–146
energy (prana), 18, 33, 81–82, 89,
104, 109, 115, 156
energy (prana) exercise, 34–35
energy awareness, 33–35
energy flow, 57–58, 109
energy sheath (pranamaya kosha),
80, 81–82, 85, 93, 121–122
engagement levels, 130–132
Enlightenment thinking, 8

exercises and practices
   alternate nostril breathing, 90–91
   designing a regular practice,
      173–174
   dropping in, 97–99
   experiencing your prana, 34–35
   letting go physical practice,
      67–68
   letting go visualization, 64–67
   ocean breathing, 91
   opening your awareness, 19–20
   opening your heart, 20–21
   skull shining breathing, 92, 156
   yoga nidra (yoga sleep), 120–124

F
false identities, 14
fear, decision making out of, 155–
   156
fire (agni), 116
fire and water (pitta dosha), 116,
   117–118, 119, 145
five bodies of awareness, 53
forceful leaders, 3

G
gunas (qualities), 118–120
gurus (removers of darkness), 149

H
habits, 12–15
health (svastha), 116
heart chakra, 86–87
"how" vs. "what", 5–6

I
illumination, 147–168
   case study (John), 157–159
   case study (Kevin), 160–165
   cocreation and, 150

   conflict between darkness and
      light, 147–149
   decision making and, 155–156
   healthy polarity and, 151–154
   internal darkness and, 151
   maintaining positive energy,
      154–155
   polarity of day and night, 151
   presence and, 149, 156–159
   reactivity to responsiveness shift,
      155–157
   removers of darkness and leader-
      ship, 149–151
   Vedic perspective on darkness
      and light, 148–149
influencing others, 15–16
inner circle of your being, 43–44
Inner Switch Leaders, xxxii, 150
inspiration, 15
integrated homeostasis, 79
integrated leaders, 112
integration, 101–124
   about, 103
   Ayurveda and, 115–120
   case study (Sandra), 107–109
   chakras and, 103
   definition, 103, 112
   disconnected leaders, 102–103
   embodied knowledge and, 105–
      106
   equanimity capacity with, 112–
      113
   importance to effective leader-
      ship, 112
   integrated beings with intention-
      ality, 101–102
   moving from practice to applica-
      tion, 120

moving from thinking and doing to feeling and being, 109–110

self-compassion in, 106–107

self-protective mechanisms preventing, 103

stages of, 110–112

when to use integration technique, 113–115

Yogic philosophy and, 104–105

intention, living with. *See* integration

intentions, setting, 110–111, 155

internal darkness, 151

internal motivators, 14

intrinsic motivation, 128–129

J

joyfulness, 6

judgmental language, 133

K

kapalabhati pranayama (skull shining breath), 92, 156

kapha dosha (earth and water), 116, 117, 118, 119, 146

koshas (sheaths), 53, 80–85, 93, 103, 120, 121–122, 124, 149

L

layers of being, 53

leadership competencies, xxx

leadership presence, xxxvi–xxxviii, 71–75

learning, 24–46

accountability in, 29

being present in leadership, 45–46

being vs. doing, 27–29

body-mind connection hallmark, 35–38

case study (Marianne), 39–41

consciousness and presence hallmark, 32–33

emotions and thought patterns and, 45

energy awareness hallmark, 33–35

inner circle of your being and, 43–44

reorienting your focus, 24–27

self-inquiring hallmark, 30–32

witness consciousness hallmark, 38–43

letting go, 47–69

about, 47–50, 54–55

being in the present, 68–69

case study (Keith), 60–62, 69

case study (Trisha), 50–51

defined, 54, 69

dropping in and, 96

exploring the edge of discomfort, 55–59

learning to let go, 63–64

physical practice of, 67–68

reactivity to responsiveness shift, 51–54

visualizing, 64–67

yoga and, 55–59

letting go visualization workout, 64–67

letting go yoga stretch, 67–68

light and darkness, 147–151

Light on Yoga (Iyengar), 89

limbs of yoga, 58, 170, 178n5. *See also* yoga

M

mental sheath (manomaya kosha), 80, 82

mind-body connection, 35–38, 76–77

mindfulness, 96
myotatic reflex, 68

N

nadi shodhana pranayama (alternate nostril breathing), 90–91
nature, basic elements of, 116
negativity, 14–15
nervous system, 24–25, 46
nondoing, state of, 79–80
nostril breathing, alternate (nadi shodhana pranayama), 90–91

O

observational awareness stage of integration, 110
observers, 14
ocean breathing (ujjayi pranayama), 91
openheartedness, cultivating, 16–17
openheartedness exercise, 20–21
opening, 1–21
    awareness, 9
    awareness exercise, 19–20
    beginner's mind in, 17–18
    being observer of your thoughts, 16
    being vs. doing, 9
    case study (Alan), 3–4
    case study (Theresa), 5–6
    case study (Vince), 17
    close-mindedness and, 12–14
    connection vs. disconnection with others, 9
    consciously managing yourself, 10–12
    cultivating openness, 3, 6
    "doing" vs. state of being of "doer", 7
    emotional intelligence and, 8
    focusing on "how" vs. "what", 5–6
    habits and, 12–15
    joyfulness and, 6
    looking inside ourselves in, 18–19
    negativity and, 14–15
    openheartedness, cultivating, 16–17
    openheartedness exercise, 20–21
    self-acceptance and influencing others, 15–16
    self-influence and, 15
    wisdom of the body and, 8–9
    work-life balance and, 4–5

P

pain, previously suppressed, 153
parasympathetic nervous system (PSNS), xxii, xxiii, 25, 57, 78–79, 89, 103, 121
past, 33
Patanjali, xxvii
physical sheath (annamaya kosha), 80–81
pitta dosha (fire and water), 116, 117–118, 119, 145
polarity, 25–26, 46, 79, 111, 121–122, 151–154
postures (asanas), 40
practices. *See* exercises and practices
prana (energy), 18, 33, 81–82, 89, 104, 109, 115, 156
prana (energy) exercise, 34–35
pranamaya kosha (energy sheath), 80, 81–82, 85, 93, 121–122
pranayama (breathing practices), 90–92, 156

pratyahara (withdrawal of the senses), 58, 103

presence. *See also* dropping in
  about being present, xxxi, xxxv
  about leadership presence, xxxvi–xxxviii
  connection relying on, 129
  consciousness and, 32–33
  dropping into, 71–76, 78, 89–90, 96–97
  illumination and, 149, 156–159
  learning to be present, 45–46, 75–76
  letting go and, 68–69
  yoga training for finding, 57
prithvi (earth), 116
psychological edge of discomfort, 56

Q

qualities (gunas), 118–120
quantum energy, 104

R

reactive leaders, 3, 13
reactive state, 156
reactivity, 130–131
reactivity to responsiveness shift, 51–54, 155–157
receiving stage of integration, 111
reflex sympathetic dystrophy (RSD), xxi–xxiii
relaxation response, xxiii
repetition, 105–106
resonance, 137–141
responding vs. reacting, 77–79
root chakra, 85–86

S

sacral chakra, 86

Seated Forward Bend, 67–68
self inquiry, 30–32
self-compassion, 106–107
self-connection, 129
self-defensive belief structures, 13
self-identification, 13–14
self-influence, 15
self-inquiring hallmark, 30–32
self-mastery, 18–19
self-regulating your inner state, 10–12
sheaths (koshas), 53, 80–85, 93, 103, 120, 121–122, 124, 149
shoshin (beginner's mind), 17–18
skull shining breath (kapalabhati pranayama), 92, 156
sleep of yoga (yoga nidra), xxiii, 112, 120–124, 175–176
sleep process, 121
solar plexus chakra, 86
somatic practice, 76
space or ether (akasha), 116
stress, 152–154
stress, releasing, 57–58
svastha (health), 116
sympathetic nervous system (SNS), xxi–xxii, 24–25, 46, 74, 78, 79, 89, 121

T

team building, 141–142
third eye (or brow) chakra, 87, 98, 112, 115, 123–124, 156
third law of motion, 104
thoughts and emotions, reciprocity of, 77–78
throat chakra, 87
traumatic situations, 153

triggered feelings, 114–115, 131

U

ujjayi pranayama (ocean breathing), 91

unhooking stage of integration, 110

Untethered Soul, The (Singer), 54

V

vata dosha (air and space), 116, 117, 118, 119, 145

vayu (air or wind), 116

Vedic elements of nature, 116

Vedic objective for communication, 133

Vedic perspective on light and darkness, 148–149

Vedic perspective on team building, 141–142

vijnanamaya kosha (wisdom sheath), 80, 82–83, 84

violent communication, 133

visualization exercise in letting go, 64–67

W

water (apas), 116

wisdom of the body, 8–9

wisdom sheath (vijnanamaya kosha), 80, 82–83, 84

witness consciousness, xxii, 38–43, 93, 123–127, 156–157

witness perspective, 57

work-life balance, 4–5

workplace bullying, 126–127

workplace disengagement, 127

workplace productivity study (2019), 127–128

workplace relationships, 128–129

Y

yoga. *See also* Ayurvedic concepts

    author's personal experience healing with, xxi–xxv

    author's yoga inspired approach to leadership, xxv–xxvi, xxviii

    benefits of, xxxiii

    eight limbs of, 58, 170, 178n5

    energy flow and, 57–58, 109

    finding presence with, 57

    inward focus yogic approach, xxvi

    leadership principles drawn from, xxxiv–xxxvi

    letting go and, 55–59

    origins, xxvii–xxviii

    philosophy of, 104–105, 170

    postures (asanas) in, 40

    practicing in business context, xxxiii

    releasing stress with, 57–58

yoga nidra (yoga sleep), xxiii, 112, 175–176

yoga nidra (yoga sleep) guided practice, 120–124

Yoga Sutras of Patanjali, xxvii, 58